SOCIAL MEDIA PRESSURE

SOCIAL MEDIA PRESSURE

Finding Peace Alongside Jesus

John Perritt

newgrowthpress.com

New Growth Press, Greensboro, NC 27401
newgrowthpress.com
Copyright © 2023 by John Perritt

All rights reserved. No part of this publication may be reproduced, stored in a retrieval system, or transmitted in any form by any means, electronic, mechanical, photocopy, recording, or otherwise, without the prior permission of the publisher, except as provided by USA copyright law.

Unless otherwise noted, Scripture quotations are taken from The ESV® Bible (The Holy Bible, English Standard Version®). ESV® Text Edition: 2016. Copyright © 2001 by Crossway, a publishing ministry of Good News Publishers. The ESV® text has been reproduced in cooperation with and by permission of Good News Publishers. Unauthorized reproduction of this publication is prohibited. All rights reserved.

Scripture quotations marked BSB are taken from The Holy Bible, Berean Standard Bible, BSB Copyright ©2016, 2020 by Bible Hub. Used by permission. All Rights Reserved Worldwide.

Scripture quotations marked by CEV are taken from The Holy Bible, Contemporary English Version®, CEV, Copyright © 1995 American Bible Society. Used by permission. All rights reserved.

Scripture quotations marked NIV are taken from THE HOLY BIBLE, NEW INTERNATIONAL VERSION®, NIV® Copyright © 1973, 1978, 1984, 2011 by Biblica, Inc.® Used by permission. All rights reserved worldwide.

Scripture quotations marked NLT are taken from the Holy Bible, New Living Translation, copyright © 1996, 2004, 2015 by Tyndale House Foundation. Used by permission of Tyndale House Publishers, Inc., Carol Stream, Illinois 60188. All rights reserved.

Cover Design: Anna Morrison
Interior Typesetting and eBook: Lisa Parnell

ISBN: 978-1-64507-310-9 (Print)
ISBN: 978-1-64507-311-6 (eBook)

Library of Congress Cataloging-in-Publication Data on file

Printed in the United States of America

30 29 28 27 26 25 24 23   1 2 3 4 5

To Brent, Joe, Michael, and Margaret.

Working alongside each of you to impart the faith to the next generation is a joy.

CONTENTS

INTRODUCTION

Each Friday during the school year, I teach Bible classes to high school students. Three of our children attend this school, so I enjoy commuting with them at the end of the week. We pray together on the drive, listen to music, talk about exciting or stressful events for the day ahead. I cherish these moments. What I don't always cherish is sitting and waiting for them to finish talking with their friends at the end of the school day so we can go home. But I need to be more sensitive to this.

Sometimes while I'm waiting in the car, I just observe teens hanging out in the parking lot. I can often laugh at some of the interactions I witness. I can reminisce about my own years of being a teenager. However, I also experience a certain amount of sadness when I observe these students. Let me explain.

Some students appear to be friendless, standing off on their own. I see the subtle longing to fit in, for a group to accept them. I also see others who seem to have everything going for them. They appear confident, happy, and secure. The parking lot scene is the typical spectrum of students that populate any high school. A mixture of students on the scale of happy, sad, confident, or less so.

Do you know what else I see everywhere? Smartphones. Rare is the time I see a student without one. Whether they're posting selfies, answering texts, laughing at a new reel, or just scrolling to pass the time, students do most everything with phone in hand.

Don't get me wrong—I have a smartphone too and it's a major part of my daily life. I can send a message of encouragement, take a picture, keep up with the news, read my Bible, listen to great music, laugh at a funny video, and countless other good things. You can too.

But, as you are well aware, sometimes our relationships with phones can cause a lot of angst and pain. Have you ever gotten a DM that destroyed your day? Or had a humiliating picture of you posted for all to see? Has someone ever sent you explicit content? If any of these things have happened to you, you know how much hurt and embarrassment can come from misuse of phones or social media.

Perhaps it's not something someone has done—it's what they've *not* done: clicked "like" on your posts or included you in the weekend hangout you now see plastered all over Instagram and Snapchat.

This book is written in response to the anxiety many of us feel through our experience with social media. In some ways the stress and loneliness can feel overt, and in some ways it's more subtle. This book uncovers many of the ways in which our relationships, mental health, and perception of the world around us can be directly affected by our choices on social media. How do we gain more peace in our lives? How do we relate more thoughtfully with others? How do we recognize if we are becoming digitally addicted? What does God have to do with any of this?

I pray that this book meets you where you are feeling hopeless, beat up, and discouraged. I pray that it starts a helpful conversation that fills you with joy, because this book is filled with gospel hope. My biggest goal is to point you to Jesus, who sees what you are going through and whose words can bring healing and change.

You may have been following Jesus for a long time, or maybe you're brand-new in your walk of faith. Or you may not be sure where you stand with God. I'm so glad you've picked up this book. If you aren't a Christian, please read along and know that the gift of Jesus is freely offered to you. If you are a Christian, I hope you see how the love of Jesus is woven throughout the pages of this book and I hope you see how this love orders your priorities, refreshes your perspective, and leads you to respond to challenges and temptations with wisdom.

I'm excited for you to get started. Know that Jesus is with you on your journey.

FIVE THINGS YOU NEED

DON'T SKIP OVER THIS SECTION! In order to have the fullest experience of *Social Media Pressure*, you're going to need a few additional things to go along with this book.

1. A Bible

Choose a translation that's easy for you to understand.

Word-for-word translations include:

- NASB (New American Standard Bible)
- ESV (English Standard Version)
- KJV (King James Version)
- NKJV) (New King James Version)

Paraphrase translations include:

- MSG (The Message)
- CEV (Contemporary English Version)
- NIRV (New International Reader's Version)
- PHILLIPS (JB Phillips New Testament)
- Da Jesus Book (Hawaiian Pidgin New Testament)

Meet-in-the-middle translations include:

- NIV (New International Version)
- CSB (Christian Standard Bible)
- NLT (New Living Translation)

If you have trouble finding the Scripture passages, use the Table of Contents in the front of your Bible to locate the book. The Bible is actually made up of sixty-six smaller books. The New Testament, which is the back half of the Bible, contains twenty-seven books. The first part of the Bible, the Old Testament, was written before Jesus came as a baby, and it contains thirty-nine books. Each of the sixty-six books of the Bible are divided up by chapter numbers, and each chapter has verses. So, if you see something like John 5:1–14, that means the passage is found in the book of John (fourth book in the New Testament), in the fifth chapter of that book, and in the first fourteen verses.

2. A Pen

I know some people do not like writing in their Bible or books, but **DO IT ANYWAY**! A big part of this book is being willing to engage with it, and not just read it. A helpful way to do that is by actually circling words, underlining sentences, *jotting down questions*, and even drawing a picture every now and then. It's also helpful to read your Bible with a pen in hand. Down the road, you can look back and see the thoughts you've jotted down, the ways you've grown, and the prayers God has answered.

3. A Quiet Place

The world is full of distractions. Even if you're in your own room, I imagine there are lots of distractions. Before you dive into *Social Media Pressure* each day, I'd encourage you to create as much of a **DISTRACTION-FREE ENVIRONMENT** as possible. Maybe that means turning on some white noise—like a fan or sound machine—so you can't hear your little brother playing his drums. Maybe that means turning off any screens or devices that are tempting you to look at them.

4. A Slower Pace

Lots of devotionals are shorter and can be read and checked off your to-do list in minutes. These devotions are intentionally designed to take longer. You're officially invited to **WALK** through this book. Please **DON'T RUN**. Each seven-day week is set up with only four devos. This allows you to miss a couple of days and not get behind. If you find it annoying to not have one to do every day, on day five or six you could reread some of the biblical passages from that week and see how Jesus meets you differently when you go back for seconds. The point is to go slow. This isn't a race; this is a relationship. One helpful practice is picking a specific time each day to engage with this book and God's Word. We walk alongside Jesus all day long, but it's helpful to actually schedule when you are going to carve out time to read and do these exercises. Most of these devos will take you somewhere between twenty to thirty minutes. When would that work best in your rhythm of life? If possible, I would encourage you to do it first thing in the morning to set the tone for your day. But if you're not a morning person and that sounds like torture, consider doing it as the last thing before you go to sleep each night. That might mean giving up some screen time, but my guess is that spending time with Jesus will allow you to experience a deeper rest than anything you'll see on your screen. But show yourself some grace too. It's okay to miss a day!

Sample Schedule (create one that works for you):

Monday - Day 1
Tuesday - Day 2
Wednesday - Whoops, I overslept! That's okay, I can do it tonight or tomorrow.
Thurs - Day 3
Friday - Day 4
Saturday - Resting today
Sunday - Weekend conversation with my Alongsider

5. An Alongsider

It might feel intimidating, but trust me on this. Muster up the courage and ask someone to go through this book alongside you. Maybe that's a friend, parent, grandparent, youth leader, coach, teacher, pastor, Young Life leader, or a sibling.

When you commit to reading it together, it gives you someone to process it with. Consider this: If a friend asked you to do a devo with them for a month, how would you feel? See? You'd be honored! **BE BRAVE** and **INVITE SOMEONE** into this journey alongside you. You'll be thankful you did. After every four days, you'll find a section called "The Weekend Conversation." This is a set of questions for you to talk through with your Alongsider. You'll be tempted to skip it and just move on to the next day. Fight that temptation. Call your devo partner (or better yet, take a **WEEKEND WALK** together) and spend some time reflecting on the past week.

WEEK 1

DAY 1: GOD'S FACE

Blessed is the one who fears the LORD *always*, but whoever hardens his heart will fall into calamity. (Proverbs 28:14, emphasis added)

QUESTION

Where are you right now? Are you inside your house, lounging in your favorite old chair? Perhaps you're in a hammock under the shade of a tree. Are you reading this before a long day of school, or while fighting off sleepiness right before bed? No matter where you are or what time of day it is, God is with you. Stop and let that sink in. Right now, this very minute, God is watching you. The Creator of all things, the One who spoke all things into existence, is in the room with you.

Does that scare you? Creep you out a little? Does it make you feel a little awkward? Or does it bring you deep comfort? Does it make you feel safe? Secure? Loved? If you are God's child, let his presence bring you comfort and rest deep in your soul. God is all about welcoming weary, stressed, confused, angry, hurt, anxious, and depressed people like you and me. But let's not get too far ahead.

While I don't know how you'll react to this truth, I do think *fear* is an appropriate response to knowing God is near. Many of us think of fear in a negative light, but biblical fear is actually a good thing. Let's find out why.

Scripture

From Genesis to Revelation, the fear of the Lord is a constant theme. I've heard it said that the word *awe* comes close to what Scripture means when discussing the fear of the Lord. When we say that something is *awesome!* that might help us grasp what's being communicated. Respect, reverence, and humility toward God are the expressions that should flow out of our understanding of this fear.

Think of how you've felt when you've seen something magnificent. This could be an epic scene from a movie, a national landmark like Yosemite, an impressive athletic feat at the Olympics. When you see something amazing, how do you feel? How do you respond? Maybe goosebumps run up your arms and the back of your neck. Maybe your jaw drops and your eyes go wide. Maybe all you can do is stay silent because the scene before you can't be matched with words. You just want to take it all in.

But don't just take my word on it, listen to what God's Word says, "For as high as the heavens are above the earth, so great is his steadfast love toward those who fear him; as far as the east is from the west, so far does he remove our transgressions from us. As a father shows compassion to his children, so the Lord shows compassion to those who fear him" (Psalm 103:11–13). The God of the Bible loves the unlovable. I don't know about you, but I can struggle to love people that are hard to love. The reality is that we were not just unlovable; we were enemies of God when he chose to love us. The more we reflect on that reality, the deeper our fear of God grows.

A friend once asked me, "Why does the Bible tell us to fear God?" I honestly didn't have a prepared answer, but the one that came to mind was, *I think the better question is, why shouldn't we fear him?* God made all things. The entire cosmos, from vast plains of grass to the tallest snow-capped mountains and the Milky Way, were literally *spoken into existence* by this God. This same God that holds all things together by the word of his power (Hebrews 1:3) gives you the very breath that's filling your lungs right now. He gives you life, and he's always with you. Fear seems to be an appropriate response to a God who is so enormous, sovereign, and powerful—yet who draws so near to us.

Story

I don't remember the exact context, but I'm pretty sure I was in sixth grade. I was hanging with a group of friends, and school had just finished for the day. Since our elementary school stopped at sixth grade, we were the upper classman and felt like we were in charge. I'm sure we were about to leave the classroom and jump on our Huffy bicycles to ride off into the sunset. We were talking about all sorts of things, and then the conversation turned to gossip. My memory is hazy, but I know we began gossiping about "Bob."[1] Being the immature sinner I was back in middle school (this isn't to say that I'm fully matured now), I was happy to jump in on the gossip.

While I don't remember the exact words of my gossip, I know I said some harsh things about Bob. Somewhere in the category of, "Bob just gets on my nerves. I can't stand him. He drives me crazy!" These comments might seem mild compared to things you've said or things that have been said about you, but we can all agree that these words are harsh and hurtful. They are words that none of us would like for others to say about us.

Well, there's another detail of this story that makes the words sting a little more.

Right after I exclaimed, "I can't stand Bob! He drives me crazy!" his mom rounded the corner into the room. Even though she wasn't in the room when I made the statement, I knew she would have been able to hear it because I had said it pretty loudly. She looked me straight in the eyes but didn't say a word. Immediately, I felt that sinking feeling in my gut. If I think about it long enough, I can still feel it today.

I'm sure my face had a look of shock and horror. It was one of those moments where I wished I could just disappear. I wanted out of that situation as fast as possible. The waves of guilt washed over me the rest of the day.

Reflecting upon this story all these years later, I feel a new weightiness because I am now a father of five children. If anyone messes with my children, a side of me emerges that no one wants to see. At the same time, if someone hurts my children, I experience a category of hurt that I never knew existed.

Thinking back on my middle-school self, while I might have simply been embarrassed because I had been caught in gossip, I sincerely believe I was grieved by the Spirit over the harsh words I uttered about someone I would've called my friend. I think what caused me the most grief was the expression on his mother's face—a mixture of hurt and justified anger. What I said about Bob was wrong even if his mother hadn't heard me, but the point is that her presence in the room made me realize the gravity of what I had said.

God's Face

Many theologians have talked about "practicing the presence of God." They are referring to the reality that God is everywhere. The theological word for this is *omnipresence*. God's omnipresence is the reason we may laugh when we read about Adam and Eve trying to *hide* from God after sinning against him in Genesis 3. Picture them darting among the innumerable trees in the garden, anxiously trying to run from the Lord, knowing they'd sinned, clumsily patching together fig leaves to cover their newfound shame. How can you hide from God? You can't. He's everywhere. Even though we may chuckle at Adam and Eve's hiding, we try to do it all the time.

Keep the simple truth of God's omnipresence in mind as you begin this devotional. I want the truth of God's presence being with you to serve as the foundation for all your interactions on social media. The verse that begins this chapter reads, "Blessed is the one who fears the Lord *always* . . ." (emphasis added).

Going back to the story of my harsh words about my friend, had I known his mother was right around the corner, I wouldn't have said such harsh things. Now, I may have *thought* them in my heart, and that would still be wrong. My actions, however, would have been changed by the knowledge of his mother's presence. The people we gossip about are not omnipresent, but the God who made those people is. He hears and sees all things. Fearing the Lord always means understanding that God is with us every waking hour and even while we sleep.

God's face sees all your interactions on social media. He sees your scrolling. He sees what you post. He sees the private messages you share. But it's much deeper than that. His power is able to see to the heart. Why do you post the things you post and look at the things you look at? He is able to see into the desires of your heart, desires you may not even be aware of. All is exposed before him.

Next time the blue light hits your eyes as you power up a device and begin scrolling, searching for something online, considering what new shows or movies the internet is buzzing about, or thinking about what to post on social media, think about God's constant presence and nearness. Every time you pick up your phone, tablet, laptop, gaming console, or begin streaming something online, remember God is with you. How might that reality change the way you use social media? How could it change what you post? What you look at? How you react to harsh things said about you? The fear of the Lord will not only be a reoccurring theme throughout this devotional, but I want it to serve as our foundational truth for this devotional.

Practice

In John 8, Jesus speaks of his Father, saying, "And he who sent me is with me. He has not left me alone, for I always do the things that are pleasing to him" (John 8:29). Jesus remembered the presence of his Father. While we can't claim that our obedience is perfect like Jesus, every Christian can celebrate the truth that God is always with them because Jesus made a way for that to be true. Rather than some random challenge or checklist, the practice for today is meant to help you imitate your brother Jesus by remembering the constant presence of God.

Many households have sticky notes lying around. If you don't, ask your parents to buy some for you. Tell them it's for this devotional and they'll probably be delighted to buy them. They come in all sorts of sizes and colors, so pick the ones you like the most.

There's some freedom to this practice, so do what you think would be most helpful. Write a statement that will remind you of God's presence. Something like—*God is with you right now. God is here. God is everywhere. God is watching*—any statement that gets at the essence of God's omnipresence. Write that phrase on as many sticky notes as you'd like; I'd suggest at least 3–5. Jot it down in print, hand-letter it in cursive, scrawl it in big capital letters, use different colored markers or plain black ink—whatever suits your style.

Once you write that statement, put the notes all over your house—with your parents' permission, of course. If you have a phone, definitely stick one on there. Stick a note on your computer screen (tape it if the note doesn't stick). Put one on your mirror in your bedroom and on your bedside table. If you're able to drive, put a note somewhere on your dashboard. Put one in the pantry or on the back door of your house. Have fun with it.

The point is to put these notes all over the place to help you practice the presence of the Lord. If you're placing these on your phone or computer, you're going to have to remove them before you use those devices. That's totally fine, but be sure to replace them once you're done. The sticky notes will eventually lose their stickiness, so you can decide whether to replace them with new notes or not. After a while, even when you stop using the sticky notes, this practice will hopefully help you remember the truth that God is with you and is worthy of your reverence and awe. Hopefully the Lord will impress this truth upon your heart for the remainder of your life. And, as the Proverb states, you will be blessed by this truth.

SONG

"Only a Holy God" by CityAlight

DAY 2: GOD'S PRESENCE

"I will not leave you as orphans; I will come to you." (John 14:18)

Question

How did you spend your time last week? Think about your classes, friends, family, church life, extracurriculars, homework, etc. How much time did you have all to yourself? Did you have any time alone? If so, how much?

Most of our lives are filled with activity. We hop in the car and race off to school, sports, work, vacation. We may often have very little time alone. It's a good thing to be in fellowship with others; we're actually created for that! At the same time, while moments of solitude are important, I think we often avoid them because we're afraid of being alone. Moments of solitude, without the constant input of lights, colors, notifications, and entertainment to consume, can amplify this feeling of being alone. Before you push back on that, let's think a bit about what Scripture says.

Scripture

If you are familiar with the Bible, you're aware of "the fall." Adam and Eve sinned against a perfect, holy, righteous, loving God. The garden they lived in was filled with perfect beauty. Adam and Eve were filled with perfect joy as they fellowshipped with their perfect Creator. Yet they rebelled against all this. Their rebellion brought every horrible emotion into existence—anxiety, depression, grief, emptiness. Their disobedience marked the beginning of physical decay—broken bones, acne, cancer, death. Every awful, sinful thought we think has its origins in Genesis 3.

The fall is the place where endless horrors find their beginning. It's where children, like Adam and Eve, actually became orphans. Their sin separated them from their loving Creator. The fact that they tried to hide from him shows us that they knew this. They could not stand to be in God's presence because they were sinful and shameful while God is perfect.

Imagine how fearful, grieved, and ashamed they must have felt while hiding amid the garden trees as God called out, "Where are you?" (Genesis 3:9). Because Adam and Eve (and we) were made to find life in fellowship with God, to be separated from him is to be alone in the truest and worst sense of the word. But God promised to make a way to adopt them through his Son (Genesis 3:15).

When we talk about the gospel, we don't always use this adoption language, but it is an accurate description of what God has done. God has adopted us as his children through the finished work of his Son, Jesus. This is why we call God our Father.

Even as believers, we are still sinful, and when we give into our sin, we live like orphans. When we forget we are loved, we live like we're alone. This is what makes the truth of John 14:18 so vital—Jesus promises not to leave us as orphans. In Christ, we are no longer alone. But the messages and images we take in make it easy to forget this truth and miss out on the hope it brings to every part of our lives.

Story

Not too long ago I saw a skit by a comedian on YouTube. The basic premise of the skit talked about ways to ruin your day (sounds hilarious, right?!). Some of the humor may be lost in writing, so it's important to state that the comedian was genuinely being funny. Part of the humor came from the fact that obviously no one wants to ruin their day. I mean, who wakes up wanting to have a bad day?

What the comedian exposed were things we do most days that may actually make our day worse without us even realizing. The first bad habit he mentioned was checking social media first thing in the morning.

Many of us feel the sting of that because it's our common practice. Maybe that's you. When you wake up, trying to blink the sleepiness away (or pulling the blanket over your head in denial that it's morning), what's the first thing you do? Do you roll over to your phone and scroll through messages or pictures? Maybe you say you'll just check your phone "real quick," only to end up scrolling for a good twenty or thirty minutes (or more). How do you feel after starting your day this way? Worried? Energized? Encouraged? Discouraged? Distracted? Is this habit helping or hurting you?

I don't reference this comedian to shame or guilt-trip you, but to help you reflect on your habits and how they affect you. If you begin your day by checking social media, is it actually hurting you? Have you been waking up to your phone for months or years without realizing how much it affects your daily thoughts? Do the images or messages you see tempt you to be envious? Do they make you think that others have it better than you, or that you're not well liked? Do you see photos that tempt you to criticize your appearance and wish you looked more like that girl, or that actor, or that guy at school? Maybe it simply fills you with a low-level sense of discouragement you're not even aware of. It just makes you feel "off" or numb to much of life.

Without a doubt, there could be positive ways you're impacted by picking up your device. Maybe you read Scriptures posted online, an encouraging quote, or some type of devotional material. All of these could be good things. However, we all know there's a lot on social media to distract us and make us feel bad: a group of friends got together without you; they're all smiling and it looks like they had a ton of fun. That guy you like took a cute picture with another girl or vice versa. The friend who told you they were busy was actually out having a good time with someone else. And these pictures are how you start your day! They can set the tone for how you think and feel throughout the rest of the day.

A Message from Social Media

Our social media feeds are referred to as such because they *feed* us many messages each day. One of the negative messages they often feed us is *you are all alone*.

No one likes you. You have no friends. You are unpopular. All of these messages fall under the umbrella lie that you are all alone. Whether the comedian intended to point it out or not, these lies are a reason why glancing at your phone first thing may ruin your day.

You are all alone is a core anxiety for every human because it attacks a core truth that God communicates to his children, a truth he has woven into the fabric of our hearts: *you are not alone because God will never leave his children.* You see, God created us to be in perfect relationship with him and others, but our sin divides us. It separates. It drives a wedge between friends and family. Our sin feeds this fear that we are alone. Satan loves to fan the flames of the lie that you are all alone.

Think about the truth we discussed in the first chapter of this devotional—God is everywhere. We talked about how this could be a fearful truth, but God's omnipresence is also an encouraging truth. In fact, throughout Scripture God promises that he is with us always, he will never leave us or forsake us, and his love is steadfast. With these truths, God pushes back on the lie that we are alone.

Think back to the Scripture at the beginning of this chapter. We were orphaned (alone) because of our sin, but now we are adopted (loved, accepted, secure) because of God's faithfulness. Take note of how often you live like you're alone. Do you think no one notices your posts? If so, what do you believe that says about *you*? And is that belief actually true? Do you believe people aren't "liking" what you share because no one likes *you*? These thoughts come from the lie that you're all alone. Begin to push back on these lies with the truth of God's Word.

One verse that always brings me comfort is this, "For you know the grace of our Lord Jesus Christ, that though he was rich, yet for your sake he became poor, so that you by his poverty might become rich" (2 Corinthians 8:9). Christ took our poverty on himself and has made us rich beyond what we can fathom. And don't simply think of richness in monetary terms. For our immediate context, think of richness relationally. Jesus has brought you into a family that has the strongest, most fulfilling relational bonds you can imagine. Loneliness can't exist in his kingdom.

Practice

This practice may be challenging for many of you. You can probably already guess what I'm going to say, so let me say it as the reverse of what the comedian stated. *If you want to have a good day, don't check your phone first thing in the morning.*

To be clear, not checking your phone first thing in the morning won't always guarantee that you have a good day. You may not check your phone all day long and still have a terrible day. That said, social media, more often than not, fosters anxiety and discouragement. Not only does our theology back this up, there's plenty of data that point to this as well.[1]

So whatever your practice is in the morning, modify it a bit. Use any of the following examples that you find most helpful:

- Wash your face, brush your teeth, get dressed for the day, grab breakfast, step outside even just for 5 minutes (as a plus, all these things may help you be on time for school, if you ever struggle with that).
- Set a timer (an old school one) to 5 minutes. See how much you can get done in that time before you look at your phone.

- Do this challenge with a friend. See who can make it the longest without looking at their phone in the morning. Maybe you can compare your screen time or number of phone pickups with your friend when you get to school? You both could keep score and the loser has to buy the winner a cup of coffee or lunch? Or just get bragging rights?
- Put your phone downstairs and/or turn it off (if it's not used as an alarm) to add one more barrier to starting your day with your phone. For that matter, invest in an old school alarm clock!
- Make your bed or tidy your bedroom floor before looking at the phone. Better yet, choose an enjoyable task that appeals to you to do before looking at the phone.

The point is, try to not look at your phone first thing in the morning, if this has been your common practice. I'll explain more later in this book, but reading the Bible first thing is always a great idea.

If you already don't look at your phone first thing in the morning, think of some other ways you can modify your phone routine. The important thing is to notice some of the ways it may be impacting you negatively. Are you feeling left out? Anxious? Discouraged by your body image? Unlovable? An awareness of your thoughts and emotions is an important step that can easily be missed. As we move along in this devotion, we will dig into those themes and practices that may be impacting you negatively and try to think of creative ways to help you.

Remember our opening verse? Jesus promised that he would not leave us alone and orphaned, and he always keeps his promises. The point of this practice is not to just have better phone habits, but to remember the presence of Jesus with you if you belong to him. And if you don't know him yet, he wants you to know him. Replace your morning scrolling with a simple prayer; ask him to help you see him in your everyday life and to show you that you are not alone.

SONG

"Child of the King" by RYM Worship

DAY 3: GOD'S CONSTANCY

And rising very early in the morning, while it was still dark, [Jesus] departed and went out to a desolate place, and there he prayed. (Mark 1:35)

Question

How do you typically wake up in the morning? Does the ear-piercing *BEEP BEEP BEEP* of your alarm jolt you out of your slumber? Perhaps the first thing you hear is one of your parents hollering at you, "Wake up!" again and again and again. Would you call yourself a morning person or do you hate the mornings?

Regardless of how you wake up, how should Christians think about the morning? Is there a certain mindset we should have? What sort of attitude should we have toward the early morning hours? As we saw in the last chapter, our start to the morning can often shape the remainder of our day. Starting the day with God's Word has the power to shape our days around truth, and therefore help us fight the lies and temptations that weigh us down.

Scripture

Imagine Jesus during his time on earth—fully God, yet fully man, physically exhausted from engaging with the masses, casting out demons, healing the sick, dealing with the Pharisees, and yet prepared to do it all again because of his love for his Father and for sinners like you and me. Between his sacrificial serving and proclamation of the good news, Jesus goes to meet with his Father in prayer. I wonder how far he had to walk and how early he had to rise to find a quiet place. Picture him walking up a hill in his sandals, knees tired and feet coated in dust from the ground he made. See him sitting under a tree and pouring out prayer to the Father.

I can't help but imagine that some of you read the above verse from Mark and rolled your eyes a little. Maybe you read the words "very early" or "while it was still dark" and thought, *Waking up at the crack of dawn?? That just sounds like torture*. For those of you who are more extroverted, you might see the words "desolate place" and picture yourself seated alone under a tree in the middle of nowhere. Perhaps that's your biggest nightmare.

Some of us roll our eyes at a verse like this because it describes *Jesus's* practice. We read it with a mindset that thinks, *Come on, this is Jesus. He's the perfect, sinless Son of God. Of course he can wake up early and pray.* The logic follows: *Jesus was perfect. I'm not. So I'm dismissed from making this my practice. I'll take twenty more minutes of sleep, thank you very much.*

While it is completely true that we aren't perfect like Jesus, we need to consider the fact that our sinless Savior was absolutely devoted to prayer as an essential part of his daily life here on earth. I know we need to be careful saying that Jesus *needed* anything because he was perfect when he walked the earth. I say this, however, because he was fully God and *fully man*. In his humanity, he needed food and sleep to survive, for example. From this verse, we see that it was infinitely important for him to be in the presence of his Father first thing in the morning. What can this teach us? We need the Word of God if we're going to walk with God and remember his presence with us. His constancy is another way to say this. Feeding on the truth of God's Word is a way to remind us that God is constantly with us. Even Jesus, when he was being tempted in the wilderness, declared that "Man shall not live by bread alone, but by every word that comes from the mouth of God" (Matthew 4:4). Just as we constantly need nourishment from food, we need to feed upon the truth of God's constant sustaining power in our lives. Think about what we miss when we neglect time alone with God.

Story

When I was in high school, I lived one mile from school. What did this mean for me? More sleep! I remember that I got my morning routine down to a science. I had my watch synced up with the tardy bell at school and knew the last minute I could sleep in before I would be late.

If I remember correctly, I had my alarm set with the knowledge that I could still hit the snooze once or twice. I would wake up, take a fast shower, eat some breakfast, brush my teeth, jump in my 1986 Ford Taurus (don't be jealous) and arrive at my first period class with my hair still wet. Often times I was sitting down as the bell was ringing. I pushed it to the limit every day and I'm pretty sure I got a tardy or two.

I look back on that and think of how miserable that sounds to me now. I didn't care back then. My harried morning was worth a few extra minutes of sleep. Now, I like to wake up slowly. Most mornings, I typically wake up early unless I've had a bad night of sleep. If I slept well, I like to wake up early, sip some coffee, journal, pray, and read God's Word.

I don't say this to sound super spiritual or pious. I say this because I don't think I can survive apart from this practice. Yes, sometimes I believe I cannot survive without coffee, but, much more than that, I cannot survive apart from hearing from my Father each day. When I do this, I'm reminded of his constancy.

While I slept in the night, he was constantly giving me life—he gave me air to breathe, lungs that were working, a heart that kept beating. As I read his Word in the mornings, he gives me eyes to see the words of the text, a brain to process what I'm reading. Reflecting on God in Word and prayer reorients my thoughts to God's constancy. It reminds me that he is faithful—every second of every day of my life.

You see, when I think back to my last-minute, super-rushed mornings in high school, I wonder where my mind was. What I mean is this: I left no time for reflection. I woke up rushing and arrived at school before I had time to pause before God. I was living as a functional atheist. If you asked me, I would have said I believed in God, but my hurried morning didn't allow my mind to even think about him. Did I give him any thanks for keeping me through the night? Thanks for the friends I interacted with at school? I was unaware of his constant care of me and lived in a way that offered me little margin to pause and reflect on this.

Quiet Time

Talk of "quiet times" or "devotions" can be associated with all sorts of negative thoughts and emotions. Sometimes we associate these times with legalism—trying to earn God's favor or check off a spiritual to-do list. Maybe we can dispel some of those negative thoughts if we think back to those early mornings Jesus had with his Father. Can you imagine the beauty of the incarnate Son of God bowing to talk to his Father? What a glorious thought our tiny minds cannot comprehend.

Think back to my questions about the morning hour. How should a Christian think about the morning? Speaking for myself, my mind is often all over the place. It can often be filled with negativity: discouragement, guilt, confusion, sadness. Maybe you struggle with this too? All these thoughts and emotions can infect my heart and mind. If I don't address these feelings with truth, I'll let them determine what I believe about myself, God, and the world around me.

Therefore, I need to still my mind and hear from God, the source of all truth and the One who loves me perfectly. Devotions are those moments each morning when God reminds me who he is and who I am. When I wake up fearful or anxious about my day, worried about that presentation or that hard conversation with my friend, I need to remember that God is faithful. He cares about the things I'm concerned with and is walking with me in the midst of them. When

I wake up feeling unlovable, remembering the way I yelled at my kids or spoke harshly toward a friend, I need to hear about God's steadfast love for me. I need to hear that God's arms are open for repentant sinners. When I wake up with real hurts from people in my life, feeling the pain of harsh criticism or gossip about me, I need to know that God works for the good of those he loves, even when we experience real pain. God's Word doesn't ignore the difficulties of fear, sin, and pain, or slap a big, shiny bow on the hard parts of life. But his Word addresses those things with eternal truth that comforts our souls and helps us cling to God as our only source of security and steadfast love.

Early morning quiet times become less of a chore when we're convinced that we cannot survive apart from them. My heart is sinful and needs to hear truth. God's Word is truth. It is medicine for a sin-sick heart. As others have said, it is God's love letter to his children. It's a reminder that he's pursuing us in the midst of our brokenness. He is faithful. He is constant in his love. That's a good reminder that you and I desperately need each morning.

Practice

In your last practice, I encouraged you to not look at your phone first thing in the morning. For this practice, I want you to look at Scripture first. This can be done in a variety of ways. I want to make this as easy as possible, so think about your current practice of morning devotional times. Do you listen to the Bible on your phone? Do you read from a physical Bible? Do you use a devotional book or journal? What about prayer? Do you take time to pray, either out loud, silently, or in written form?

If you don't currently have a devotional or Bible-reading time, start with *one verse* each day. Don't try to start with something bigger. Ease your way into it. Think of a way in which you're consistently discouraged or a lie you consistently believe, and then find a truth from God's Word that speaks to that. If you need help, talk to your parents or a pastor. Write one verse on a notecard and take some time to read it in the morning. If you're not sure where to start, go to the Psalms. These are honest prayers toward and about God. Start with Psalm 1 (which is all about the power and benefit of meditating on God's Word).

If you typically have your devotional time in the evening, let me encourage you to find a few minutes in the morning. As I mentioned, our mornings often set the course for our day, so using them to reflect on God's truth first is an important practice for believers. It is not wrong or less meaningful to have a quiet time in the evening, but starting your day with God's Word can give you truth to remember as the day goes on as you face different challenges.

My intent for this practice is not to burden you. You know your days, your lifestyle, your family, and your weekly routines much better than I do, so think about this in a way that fits your context best. At the very least, I simply want you to think about your mornings and how some different practices might help God's truth speak into your heart and shape your day differently than when you start with your phone. When you're tempted to just hit the snooze button, picture your Savior Jesus retreating to be alone with the Father, and know that Jesus longs to meet with *you*. Remember, because God is constant, he is already there waiting to meet you when you come to his Word. You don't have to *hope* he will show up. He is already right there.

SONG

"10,000 Reasons" by Matt Redman

DAY 4: GOD'S COMFORT

You keep track of all my sorrows. You have collected all my tears in your bottle. You have recorded each one in your book. (Psalm 56:8 NLT)

Question

Right now, this very second, how do you feel? Happy? Sad? Distracted? Excited to start the day? Tired because you're at the end of a long day? Pause and really think about this. How do you feel?

The older I get, the more difficulty I have answering the question "How are you?" If you really stop and think about it, this is a complex question to answer. The reality is, life can be hard. Plans get cancelled. Loved ones pass away from old age, illness, accidents. We experience rejection from people we love. We feel alone. Maybe you're familiar with the stinging tears and the lump in your throat when sadness threatens to overwhelm you. While there are many eternal encouragements from God's Word, Christians can still be discouraged at times.

Whether you've expressed grief and sadness through tears or not, the above verse promises encouragement in the midst of a genuinely discouraging reality. For example, if you are in the midst of a really difficult disagreement with your friends, God is still loving you. He may not remove that difficult situation for weeks, months, years, or ever, but he remains faithful, even if our circumstances say otherwise.

Scripture

One of the many blessings of God's Word is the fact that it doesn't pull any punches. It doesn't sugarcoat the difficulties of life. You don't have to read too much of the Bible before you come across all sorts of sorrows. Murder, incest, rape, and drunkenness are in some of the earliest chapters of the Bible. Cain murders his own brother. Noah gets drunk and passes out (after being gloriously delivered by God from the flood, no less!). Job loses everything—his family, his possessions, his health—in the blink of an eye. The Egyptians enslave and oppress the nation of Israel. David commits adultery and then has a man killed to cover up his own sins. Why would I call these stories a blessing?

To be clear, I am not saying that these horrible occurrences are blessings. The blessing comes from the fact that God's Word prepares us for sorrows in this life. To say it another way, we shouldn't be surprised by suffering in this world because the Bible tells us we should expect it. More than that, God is not surprised by suffering, and he won't let it have the last word in the lives of his people. This is a great comfort. Though suffering grieves him, it does not catch him off guard or thwart his promise to work all things for the good of those who love him.

In the psalm above, David writes about his "sorrows" and "tears." Even though we clearly see sadness from this psalm, it should bring much comfort. Why? Well, at the very least, the psalm teaches us sorrow and tears are a normal part of this fallen world. This means that if you feel sorrow, nothing is wrong with you. Sadness is the right response to God's good design being warped and affected by sin. We were created for a perfect existence, so our souls are grieved when they witness the brokenness of this world. Therefore, it is normal to be sad in a sinful world.

Story

Episode 5 of The Gospel Coalition podcast, *Recorded*, is entitled "Scrolling Alone." The description reads:

> In 2009, about a quarter of American high school students said they had "persistent feelings of sadness or hopelessness." By last year it was up to 44 percent, the highest level of teenage sadness ever recorded.
>
> For girls, the rate rose to 57 percent. That means more than half of teenage girls feel persistently sad or hopeless. If you stood a teen from 2009 next to a teen from 2022, what would be the most noticeable difference between them? One of them would be on her phone.[1]

In the episode, Sarah Eekhoff Zylstra shares stories of young women who are being shaped by social media. Let me state the obvious: sadness existed before phones. Many tear-filled tissues were used long before social media was even a concept. That said, what is it about our phones and social media that seems to be increasing the sadness and sorrow of life in a fallen world?

To be sure, there are many answers to that question. Being excluded from a group of people has always been a part of life in a fallen world, but social media allows you to see pictures of it firsthand. Comparison is a natural bent of our sinful hearts, but social media enhances that even more. Body image issues for guys and girls have taken on new life when they surface through social media. Suffice it to say, whoever you are, you have felt some sadness as a result of social media. Sometimes you may not even be able to pinpoint why you feel sad—you just do.

Teenagers (like all humans) have always been sinful, but social media has now given them a new avenue to express their sinfulness. Think of it this way—bullies have always bullied people in the school hallways, but now social media has created new outlets for bullying. In a matter of seconds, anyone can re-share an embarrassing video of another person, or screenshot a mean-spirited text about someone else. Anonymous social media platforms have even allowed harsh words to be uttered by people who may have held back if they were face-to-face. Take comments on a public social media post, for example. They run the gamut from insensitive to arrogant to downright vicious: *She's such an idiot! Clearly you don't know what you're talking about. He must have no life. Talk about UGLY!* Can you imagine someone saying these to another person's face? I hope not, but they're no less stinging and painful when they're typed from behind the shelter of a screen. And when they're directed at us, the pain is all too real.

Subtler forms of bullying have also come about because of social media. Intentionally leaving people untagged from a photo to make them feel left out. Sharing pictures of a fun party with the *desire* that the uninvited will see it and feel lesser because of it. The point is that our hearts are sinful and will think of creative new ways to express their sinfulness through social media.

The Sorrows of Social Media

Some of the examples above might reflect sorrows you've personally experienced through your social media usage. Truth be told, what you've experienced may be too extreme to share in a book like this. Here's what I want you to know—Jesus sees your sorrow. Hebrews 4:14–16 tells us that we worship a Savior who knows what we are going through. He is a Savior who entered into a sorrow-filled world, out of his love for his Father and for his children.

Let's get more specific. Think of a particular example of a time when you were hurt through social media. (Stop and try to pull up a specific memory.) Did someone mock your appearance, talents, intellect, maybe even your faith? Now, think about the fact that Jesus saw that. He knows your hurt. He knows how it feels, because not only is he God, who knows everything, but because when he was on earth "he was despised and rejected" (Isaiah 53:3). He doesn't just know *about* your hurt—he experienced it to the utmost.

Thinking back to Psalm 56 that opened this chapter, there isn't one tear spilt over social media that's forgotten by your Savior. As I said, you may feel sadness when you're scrolling and you may not even know why. But God knows.

In that same psalm, David goes on to say, "This I know, that God is for me. . . . in God I trust; I shall not be afraid. What can man do to me?" (Psalm 56:9, 11). The sorrow David experienced didn't turn into bitterness but confident hope. He knew that his God didn't forget his tears with a dismissive, *Shake it off. It'll be okay*, or an empty, *Cheer up.* David's God said, *I see your pain. I hear your sorrow.*

This truth gets back to the earlier blessing of God's Word that I mentioned. The Bible doesn't sugarcoat sorrow, but it also doesn't give some cheap form of comfort either. God acknowledges the real hurt, the real pain, and the real tears of this life and he says, *I see it. I saw my Son hanging on the cross to heal it*. God says he counts our tears because he counted the cost of what it meant to take on flesh and walk this earth. Jesus was ridiculed, questioned, spit on, abandoned, beaten, and tempted in every way, yet without sin (Isaiah 53; Hebrews 4:15). He wept over death as well as rebellion (John 11:35; Luke 13:34). He was, and is, no stranger to sadness. He is not some distant or casual observer of your suffering.

When you become a parent, you learn there are new pains you never knew existed. Those pains are the pains of your children. When a child hurts, there's a real sense in which the parent may be hurting worse. What about our heavenly Father? When he sees his children hurt, he does not stand at a distance unmoved by their pain. Whatever pain you have right now, please know that the God of the Bible cares deeply for you. Cry out to him and ask him to help you see and believe that truth. Know that he hears you.

Practice

During the Sermon on the Mount, when Jesus talks about anxiety, he tells the people to look at creation (Matthew

6:25–34). Look at the birds, look at the flowers, and see how God is caring for these things. As Jesus says, if God cares for these things, how much more will he care for his children, who are of *much* more value?

Let's take Jesus's instruction here seriously. I think this might be the easiest practice you've had so far. It might end up being the easiest in the book. Here's what I want you to do. Go outside. That's it. Just go outside. If it's too hot or too cold or raining or snowing and you don't feel like it, just look out the window.

What do you see when you look outside? Old, green trees stretching up to the sky? Sunlight sparkling on a body of water? The moon casting light and shadows on the lawn? Animals? What kinds of animals? Gray squirrels flitting around trees? Your neighbor's dog running through the yard with a stick? How many kinds of birds can you see, and what are they doing? Take note of what you see. Either write it down or just take a mental note of it. But take time to really look at the detail. Ask God to open your eyes and see what he has made and how he cares for and sustains it.

In essence, when you find yourself giving into anxieties or sadness, look at God's book of creation and how he cares for it. He is speaking to us. Psalm 19 says "the heavens declare the glory of God, and the sky above proclaims his handiwork." Whether you sit outside, go for a walk, or look out the window, see the hand of your Creator. There's not a human that created the animals you see outside. There's no group of engineers that put all the stars in the sky. Even the houses and forms of transportation you may behold—anything man-made—still has its origins in the Creator of the brains, hands, feet, etc. that made those created things. See the hand of your Creator in *everything*.

He knows all the types of trees in your yard and how many leaves are on each tree. If you can see an ocean from where you live, he knows how many gallons of water your eyes can see. He knows the number of stars outside your window. And even though he is so big, holy, and glorious, he cares for you personally (Psalm 8). Let this practice move your eyes to the glory of your good God, who cares for you in your suffering.

SONG

"Wonderfully Made" by Ellie Holcomb

THE WEEKEND CONVERSATION

1. Which day stuck out to you the most and why?
   ❒ GOD'S FACE
   ❒ GOD'S PRESENCE
   ❒ GOD'S CONSTANCY
   ❒ GOD'S COMFORT

2. Have you begun to think differently about your phone usage and social media habits? If so, how? Have you noticed the different ways your emotions are affected by your social media habits?

3. Share a few of your thoughts or questions either about social media or the Bible. Consider sharing a concerning habit you have with your social media usage.

4. Did you experience any moments of sorrow this week (social media related or otherwise)? Can you reflect on ways that God met you in your moment of need?

5. How has your growing awareness of God's presence and faithfulness affected the way you use your phone and the way you approach social media?

6. Which of the Practices did you enjoy most? Which helped you to connect with Jesus?

7. Which song and/or lyric did you most resonate with? Why?

8. How can your Alongsider be praying for you?

WEEK 2

DAY 1: OTHERS HAVE

"You shall not covet your neighbor's house;
you shall not covet your neighbor's wife, . . . or anything
that is your neighbor's." (Exodus 20:17)

Question

Do you ever remember your dreams? Maybe you've dreamt you could fly, soaring over the ocean, through tunnels, or above the clouds. Or maybe you dream of a life of fame, singing your own songs on a huge stage as the crowd roars and sings along. Maybe you dream of luxury vacations, of being a spy on some critical mission, or of eating the most decadent meal.

In one of my recurring childhood dreams, I remember getting a bunch of toys—Transformers, to be specific. I dreamed I not only got all the new Transformer toys, but, if memory serves me correctly, I got *all* the Transformer toys that were *ever created*. It was so awesome! It was so real.

Then, I woke up. No toys. All the excitement from the dream disappeared, just like the toys. Disappointment replaced joy. It sincerely hurt to wake up from those dreams. Devastation would be an accurate description of my emotions.

Scripture

I'm no expert on dreams, but I know they can often line up with our desires. This isn't always a good thing. Not all desires are bad, but some are. Desires are bad when they are for sinful things, *or* when we desire good things *too much*—so much that we think we can't live or have real joy without them. They can be longings for things we don't have, and these longings can turn into discontentment and covetousness. God's command against covetousness is the loving caution he gives us in the tenth commandment, listed above.

Anytime we think about the Ten Commandments, the order is so important. And I'm not simply talking about the order of the commandments themselves. Here's what I mean—God saved his people first, *then* he gave them the commandments. He did not say, "Obey these commandments and then I might save you." He began the commandments by saying, "I am the LORD your God, who brought you out of the land of Egypt, out of the house of slavery" (Exodus 20:2). In essence he's saying, *I love you as a Father and have saved you; now live this way*. So, as we think about obeying God's commandments, we must remember that we obey from a place of security in God's love, not to *earn* God's love.

Story

I can vividly remember a specific recess from my elementary days at school. Recess was always fun because you could go wherever your imagination took you. You would race out to the playground and start participating in something that drew your attention. Or you just followed your friends and began playing whatever game you all came up with. Whether it was tag, red rover, hide-and-seek, football, or any other game—recess provided the opportunity. It was glorious. (I'm sure the teachers enjoyed the break from the students as well.)

On this particular day, I was playing on the playground when something grabbed my attention. It was the sound of people chanting a fellow classmate's name. As I looked in the direction of the chanting, I noticed it was a group of girls chanting a boy's name. They were chanting as he spun them around on the merry-go-round. It seemed like every push of the merry-go-round only increased their enthusiasm for his amazing talent on display. I'm sure there were ten or so girls on the merry-go-round, but it seemed like an arena of young girls enamored with his gift of merry-go-round . . . ness?

As you can imagine, I didn't sit back and smile at his accomplishment. I didn't think, *Good for him. Look at all those girls loving him. So glad he's having such a good day.* I'm sure I thought something along these lines: *I can do better than that. Just wait until they see what I can do.* So I walked over to the merry-go-round and gently pushed this boy aside to display my merry-go-round spinning skills. Once they witnessed me in action, I knew the young ladies would be impressed by my technique. I knew my name would become the new chant of these girls. I was so ready for the glory I was about to receive.

To my surprise, they weren't impressed. In fact, they began chanting the other boy's name again. It was as if my actions only renewed their vigor to chant his name. They actually booed me as I took the wheel of the merry-go-round. At first I thought, *Well, they just weren't impressed by my first push. Let me try again . . . and again . . . and again.* But they weren't swayed. They didn't think I was as awesome as I thought. So I did what any rational little boy would do, and quietly walked away.

I wish that's what I did, but it wasn't. I punched him in the face. To my shame, I punched him square in the nose.

I remember running away but then trying to gather my composure and think of my next move. I had enough presence of mind to know that I only had a matter of time before word would get out about the assault I had just committed on the playground. I knew he would make his way to our teacher, so I had to get to her first. I walked over to her to distract her. I'm not sure what my exact plan was. Did I think I could win her over too—maybe make her like me enough to think I was innocent? I don't know what I was thinking, but I remember seeing the boy walking toward us. I knew my time was limited, so I began using some of my best jokes on the teacher. Maybe add some levity to the scenario? I don't know. Keep in mind that if this seems like a completely illogical plan, it's because it was hatched from the mind of a kid that just punched another kid in the face.

As the uniquely-gifted, merry-go-round kid walked up (bloodied) and interrupted my comedy routine, the teacher was obviously surprised. I futilely tried to match her surprise and display the best shocked expression I could muster. Maybe my shocked expression could convince her of my innocence? As the teacher and I both looked in horror and curiosity, wondering what events could have caused this disaster, everything soon came to light. I was guilty. I got in trouble. I'm pretty sure we hugged, and I asked for forgiveness. And to this day, I don't go near merry-go-rounds.

Poisoned Hearts

The little heart I had on that playground is the same heart I'm carrying around today. By God's grace, my heart is redeemed and is being conformed more into the likeness of Jesus, but it's still poisoned with sin. Sadly, it's not just poisoned with one specific sin, but many.

Just like it was that day so many years ago, my heart is a covetous one. I wanted the glory that the other boy had. I wanted the admiration of others. In short, I wanted his life. Do you ever feel that way? Of course, you do.

While you might not use the word *covetous*, you may be more familiar with the word *jealous*. Both words are associated with the more recent term *FOMO*, the fear of missing out. FOMO represents the anxiety of missing out on any opportunity or experience that might make us happier or bring us joy. It can also be a sign of covetousness, showing us that we think we must have what someone else has in order to be happy or satisfied.

This fear can be the reason why we endlessly scroll social media. Not only do we want to remain aware of what's happening in the broader culture, but we want to know what all our friends are up to. *Is there a party I don't know about? I've heard they like each other, are they together right now? I have such a crush on this person, what are they up to?*

The fear of missing out gets at our longings for what other people have. *Their life is so much better than mine. I wish I had their body. I wish I looked the way they look. Their clothing/car/house/vacation/etc. is so much nicer than mine. My life is pathetic in comparison.*

God's command against covetousness displays his knowledge of our fallen hearts. He knows that our sin tries to convince us that someone else has it better than we do. As we will discuss more later, our heart often lies to us, and this is one lie it tells us: *all the people you look at on social media have a better life than you. They're happier, better looking, more fulfilled, more successful. You'll never measure up or have that kind of happiness.*

You see, at the root of covetousness is doubt about God's goodness. The life you have is a grace from God. Whatever you have in life—house or apartment, car or no car, talents, health, education, etc.—they are gifts from the Lord. We may never know why some people seem to have more than us, but we do know that the God of the Bible is a good God. In Romans 8:28, we are told that no matter what difficulty we may be facing, we have a God who is working good for his own children. Through the good and the bad, we have a loving God. A faithful God. A generous God who loves to give gifts. FOMO makes us miss the goodness of God in our own lives.

Please know that I'm not saying that you don't have real hurts from things you've missed out on, or that someone else's life might even have been easier than yours. I'm not making light of that. More importantly, God isn't either. Our hearts weren't designed to miss out on true joy. We were designed to share in perfect fellowship with God and others. Sin, however, has brought about a separation between people and God—so some of our fears of missing out are valid. The hurt is legitimate. Sadly, we will miss out in this life. And Jesus wants you to take those hurts to him. You can voice them to him and know that he cares.

At the same time, we must be careful. While being left out is a painful reality, we must be cautious when our hearts move to covetous discontentment in response to missing out. Not only do coveting and discontentment cause us pain and misery, but they also move us to doubt God's faithful provision of the life he has given us.

God is asking us to trust him. He acknowledges the real pain associated with missing out in this life—whatever that may look like. But he wants you to see the blessings he's bestowed on your life through the work of Jesus. He wants you to see the goodness he's lavished on you not only in your current life, but also in the life to come. The best of this life is a shadow of the next life. In Christ, the Bible tells us:

- God has promised to be with you always (Matthew 28:20).
- God has given you every spiritual blessing in the heavenly places (Ephesians 1:3).
- God says that those who follow him are adopted into a family and have received spiritual mothers, fathers, sisters, and brothers (Matthew 12:50).
- You are securely and eternally loved, and no one can change that (John 10:27–28).
- Jesus is preparing a place for you (John 14:2–3).
- Jesus will supply all your needs (Philippians 4:19).
- Jesus delights to give you good gifts (Luke 11:13).

In the midst of feeling left out or not having something that you desire, consider how Jesus meets you where you are. Jesus knows what it's like to be excluded. He knows what it means to not fit in. When you're tempted to covet what others have, move your eyes to see the riches you do have in Jesus.

Practice

I think this will be a fun practice for you; I hope it will. I want you to get together with a group of friends. Three, five, ten—as many friends as you'd like to get together with. Walk around an outdoor mall, eat at a restaurant, watch a movie, walk on a nature trail—whatever sounds like fun for you and your friends.

Here's the challenge: leave your phones behind.

Of course, be sure to let your parents know you may be without your phone for a time (if they want you to have your phone with you, consider turning it to airplane mode or silencing notifications). The challenge is to do something fun with a group of friends without sharing it on social media. Don't take any pictures. Or if you do take pictures, don't share them through social media. Don't comment about it online after the fact. Just share it in real time with the people you're with. Be in the moment!

This should be a screen-free night with your friends. If it's an hour, that's good. If it's several hours, even better. Just be in each other's presence without the pressure to show others what you're doing. Enjoy each other's company without thinking about what others might be doing at the same time. Ask Jesus to help you be present and aware of the good gifts he has given you. Have fun!

Song

"My Lighthouse" by Rend Collective

DAY 2: OTHERS' HAPPINESS

It made me jealous to see proud and evil people and to watch them prosper. (Psalm 73:3 CEV)

Question

Do you ever struggle to be happy for others? When someone comes up to you and shares something exciting that's happening to them, is there a little part of you that's bothered? I know I never struggle in this way, but maybe you do. Just kidding! I totally struggle with this, and I would assume you might from time to time. If you don't, praise God for the fact that you don't struggle in this way.

Picture this: you walk into school or church, ready for another normal day, nothing particularly exciting planned. Your best friend bounds up to you, smiling uncontrollably, and shares some news. Fill in whatever makes sense to you: "I got the lead in the spring musical!" Meanwhile, you didn't even get in the show. "I made it onto the football team!" Meanwhile, you got cut during tryouts. "I got a new phone for my birthday!" You're still using an old model that's outdated and *slow*. "He finally asked me out!" You've never even been asked on a date.

How do you respond to this good news? Your friend is excited about the good things happening in their life. If you were in their shoes you'd be excited too, but maybe you find it hard to be as happy as they are when you hear their news. You stop yourself from scoffing and try to suppress the annoyance boiling up inside. Or maybe when your friend leaves, you fight back tears of frustration over your own life, which feels boring at best. Maybe you feel like a failure or maybe you feel angry, feeling entitled to the same blessings your friend has.

In the previous chapter we looked at our covetousness, but I want to dig into that a little more. Why does our sin make it hard for us to share in other people's joy? Why do we get annoyed, sometimes, at other people's happiness?

Scripture

Through the years, the Lord has grown me to see the beauty of God's Word. One part of God's Word I've grown to love is the book of Psalms. I love how the Psalms capture emotions, and I love their honesty. I love how the Psalms say what some of us are, at times, too afraid to admit. I also love that they help put words to what I'm often unable to voice.

Read the opening verse again. The psalmist is jealous to see all these wicked people living the good life. They have success, money, good health, material prosperity. Do you ever look at the world and think, *They have it so easy. They have so much money and freedom. God, I'm trying to faithfully serve you and what am I getting in return? I'm following you but my life is harder than theirs!*

If you read the entirety of Psalm 73, you'll see that the psalmist comes to his senses and sees the Lord's goodness. He also sees that the good life he thinks others have isn't really all that it seems. It won't even last. What we see on the surface may not reflect what is actually true.

Story

I don't know if this is true of your family, but in my family, we have arguments. Sometimes those arguments occur when we're getting ready for church on Sundays. There are even times when an argument begins at home and then continues on the drive to church, right up to the very second we open the car doors in the church parking lot.

Of course, we exit our vehicle in an orderly fashion, dressed in our neat Sunday clothes, smiling at our fellow church members, looking like a "good Christian family." From the outside, you might never guess that we'd just been fighting. We file into church looking like we've got all our ducks in a row. I've often thought, *John, you're such a liar. You were screaming at your children seconds ago and now you're singing to the glory of God.*

I assume our family isn't the only family that's had those moments. Let me remind all of us that church is the exact place we need to be after those difficult family arguments. We must reject the lie that the family who fights doesn't belong in church. Church is a great place to take your brokenness to be healed. Despite how things may look on the surface, let's reject the lie that every family at church is all smiles. Their house is broken too.

The Earth Is Groaning

In Romans 8:22 we read, "For we know that the whole creation has been groaning together in the pains of childbirth until now." In a recent episode of *The Local Youth Worker* podcast, author Melissa Kruger commented that she keeps this verse in mind as she scrolls through social media. She remarked that, although this may seem like a strange verse, it reminds her that everyone's "highlight reel" doesn't necessarily reflect reality.[1] In other words, they're groaning too.

Many of us are familiar with this highlight reel—all the good parts of people's lives that make their way onto social media. They only show the good, not the struggles. A cute selfie with our significant other from last week (ignoring the fight we just had with them and the harsh remarks we made). The perfect family Christmas with fresh baked cinnamon rolls and matching plaid pajamas (okay, maybe some of you wouldn't be caught dead wearing matching family pajamas). The point is we show the good stuff. No pain. No heartache. No groaning. Only prospering, like the psalmist observed. Even when people decide to be "authentic" about their hardships on social media, they're still choosing what to share. We're still not seeing the full picture of their lives. Add to that the fact that their "authenticity" can often be a form of manipulation, which simply tries to win sympathy or favor from their followers.

The highlight reel is another aspect of the anxiety associated with FOMO. We can't help but compare our behind-the-scenes brokenness and boredom with the perfection others seem to possess. We know how imperfect our lives are, but we tend to think others have it all together. On the outside, others seem to escape the pains of this fallen world.

To fight this FOMO, we may be tempted to try and play the game. We end up creating our idea of perfection. We begin to curate our own highlight reel. We start to share and post the best parts of our lives. Just the vacations, concerts, and experiences we know others want. We show the game-winning shot we just made, the impressive cake we just baked, the amazing sunset we witnessed, that hilarious viral challenge that gets a lot of likes, and the moment when we were with the in-crowd.

Some of this can be totally fine and innocent. We may simply be inviting people to share in the joy of what we have witnessed or created. At the same time, we need to be honest with our own hearts. Are we being lured into the trap of the highlight reel?

Are we trying to make others jealous? Are we attempting to push back on our sadness by making others think we have the good life? Will their "liking" and seeing what we're up to give us just enough happiness to smother the groanings of this life? Obviously, this isn't the solution, but sometimes we think it is because it feels good and gratifying in the moment. So what is the *real* solution?

The solution is to look at any image on social media through the lens of Scripture. Behind every smile, sunset, and party is the groaning of creation for the return of Jesus. Think about it, Jesus is above all things. He is the Light of the World, the Bread of Life, the source of Living Water, the Resurrection and the Life, the Good Shepherd who lays down his life for the sheep. At God's "right hand are pleasures forevermore" (Psalm 16:11). This world, especially in its broken, sinful state, cannot compare to the fulfillment and joy of knowing Jesus and being with him and the Father in heaven. Even the best parts of this life aren't enough to give us lasting, complete joy. Don't misunderstand me and think I'm encouraging you to take joy in the fact that everyone is suffering—that's not the point at all.

In the midst of your sadness, know that you are not the only one struggling. Every human—no matter how rich, how smiley, how beautiful—is longing for another life. Pray that you can share in the joy others share through social media, but know that their life is just as broken as yours, and that they are in need of the same Savior you are. We need to remember this truth as we come across other people's happiness on social media, but there's also a second truth to remember: our own sinful heart.

There's a part of us that's simply jealous of other people's happiness. Therefore, when you see someone else's highlight reel or happiness, ask God to help you have sincere joy for them. Even when you think someone may be posting something to make you feel less-than, pray that you won't judge their motives, but will truly share their happiness with them. And remember that both your ultimate happiness and theirs won't be found in the experiences and blessings of this world, but in Christ. We need him to lift our eyes to himself, to help us believe that he is the source of true, lasting "fullness of joy" (Psalm 16:11).

For many of us, this challenge to be selfless and content is impossible—and that's exactly the point. Truth be told, we cannot judge other people's posts perfectly, and we often can't help but be jealous of what others have. And that's exactly why we need Jesus.

Jesus always took joy in the good things people took pleasure in. Jesus has compassion for judgmental and jealous hearts like yours and mine. By his grace, he wants us to fight those natural impulses in our hearts, but he also wants us to fight against the lie that those impulses are irredeemable. Rest in the reality that Jesus welcomes restless hearts. He offers compassion and forgiveness to the judgmental.

Practice

The highlight reel of social media is a real struggle for most of us. I want you to turn that struggle into an opportunity to pray. See my explanation and example below. Please feel free to modify the following prayer to fit the specific post, but it's important to keep some form of this outline in place.

First, **catch** yourself in your possible temptation. When you see a friend's photo from their vacation or with their significant other, how do you feel? Angry? Jealous? Grumpy? Discouraged? Take note of how you respond and whether your response reflects a heart of envy or discontentment. Ask God to help you do this. Second, appropriately **compare** your life to theirs. Remind yourself that what you're seeing is just a glimpse of their life and they may be struggling in ways you can't see. And no matter what material things they have, Jesus is the only source of eternal and all-satisfying joy. Third, practice **compassion** toward others. Pray that God would help them where they are struggling. Pray that he would help them find their ultimate joy in him. Lastly, practice true **community** by sharing in their joy. Find ways to rejoice with them. Thank God for the blessings he has given them. Practice this in your heart and mind, but don't just keep it to yourself. Encourage them and celebrate with them in person, or comment on their photo to show them you are excited for them.

So when you come across someone's highlight reel on social media and you're tempted to judge or despair, ask the Spirit to help you pray something along these lines:

- CATCH: Father, I'm tempted to be jealous of their life and circumstances. I'm tempted to be discouraged because I don't have what they have. I'm tempted to compare. It feels like their life is happier than mine because of what they have.
- COMPARE: Help me know they are struggling in ways I am not aware. Help me realize they are struggling in many of the same ways I am. Guard me from taking joy in the fact that they are struggling.
- COMPASSION: Help me to have a compassionate heart like Jesus for them. Please help them in their specific sorrows. Help them with their struggles. Please give them wisdom for their circumstances and give them joy in You.
- COMMUNITY: Father, help me share in their joy. Help me delight in what they're posting if it's something appropriate. Help me to remember to encourage them the next time I see them and to foster a Christlike compassion for my peers.

SONG

"Brand New" by Ben Rector

DAY 3: OTHERS' HARSHNESS

"None is righteous, no, not one; no one understands; no one seeks for God. All have turned aside; together they have become worthless; no one does good, not even one." (Romans 3:10–12)

Question

Wouldn't you like to get an artistic painting or sketch of the above verses framed on your wall? Picture a serene landscape like the beach at sunset with these words plastered over top of it and hung up on the wall. Maybe display it near your front door for all your guests to see. As they walk in, you can just scowl and point to those verses while shaking your head in disgust and judgment.

Okay, please don't do that. In no time you'd have fewer and fewer visitors coming over, and I just don't want that on my conscience.

Scripture

When most people outside the church hear or read verses like these from Romans 3 (which are actually quotes from the Psalms) they probably react negatively. They feel judged. They may think that Christians believe these verses describe everyone outside the church and cling to them with a self-righteous attitude.

Not only do Christians believe these verses speak about their *own* hearts, they react (or should react) differently than the world might expect. True believers should read these verses and be humbled. They read these verses with conviction of their own sin and with gratitude for Jesus and his sacrifice on their behalf. But while these verses should humble us first and foremost, they should also shape our view of human nature and the painful interactions we experience in friendships and through social media.

Story

Let me tell you a true story of two friends (I've changed the names)—Trevor and Nathan. They do just about everything together. They hang out at school and do homework together in the library, sit near each other in class (trying not to get caught cracking jokes), drive around after school most days listening to their favorite bands, and hang out at their favorite coffee shops on the weekends. Rare is the weekend when they don't hang out.

Gradually, however, Trevor notices that Nathan is spending less time with him, doing things with others without inviting Trevor along, responding to texts with greater and greater delay. He sees Trevor down the hall in school but barely acknowledges him with a wave. He starts sitting next to other friends at lunch and barely talking to Trevor in class. Time together decreases and excuses increase.

Then, Nathan starts sending Trevor photos of himself with his other friends. Playing paintball, going to football games as a group, hanging out at the coffee shops where Trevor and Nathan used to hang out together. Nathan snaps a photo with these other friends and texts it to Trevor with the words *Miss you, man!* Trevor slumps in his chair, annoyed and discouraged. He can't help but wonder, *If you miss me so much, why didn't you invite me along? If you really miss me, why aren't you treating me like a friend anymore?*

Difficult Relationships

Relationships are incredibly hard. They have been since Genesis 3, and they will continue to be hard until Jesus returns. Social media and phones, however, have now made relationships even harder! Just like so many other difficulties in this fallen world, phones and social media have now added a layer of complexity.

We can look to the above example of Trevor and Nathan as evidence of this, but there are also subtle forms of this that permeate our daily lives. Some of these strains on relationships have become so common that we don't even think about them. How many times have you been at a restaurant with a dear friend and in mid-conversation they pick up their phone or glance at their smartwatch? You know they love you and care about you, but you also know they just gave their attention to something else while you were talking. This is so everyday and commonplace, we don't even think to question it anymore. We've simply learned to accept it. This is just one minor example of the relational strain our devices can foster in our lives.

But, let's zoom in a bit more on the text exchange between Nathan and Trevor. Nathan hangs out with other friends, snaps a picture, and texts it to Trevor (who isn't invited) with the caption, "Miss you, man!" I think Nathan is being thoughtless at best. Perhaps he snaps the photo and sends it with very little thought as to how it might be received. To be blunt, though, I think Nathan is trying to foster jealousy, hurt, or discouragement. At the very least, he is manipulating his other friends by using them to hurt Trevor. Think of what a contrast there is between Nathan's behavior and how Scripture describes friendship and community:

- "Through love serve one another" (Galatians 5:13). Are Nathan's actions loving? Are they done in service to his friend or himself?
- "Outdo one another in showing honor" (Romans 12:10). Is Nathan honoring his friend through his behavior?
- "Do nothing from selfish ambition or conceit, but in humility count others more significant than yourselves" (Philippians 2:3). Who is Nathan treating as more significant—himself or his friend Trevor? Is Nathan acting out of selfishness or selflessness?

The Bible not only shows us what relationships should look like, but it also vividly portrays the way human relationships break down and become destructive. Romans 3, as well as all of Scripture, paints a picture of humanity that isn't rosy. The passage continues, "Their throat is an open grave; they use their tongues to deceive. The venom of asps is under their lips. Their mouth is full of curses and bitterness" (Romans 3:13–14).

I don't think it's misapplication to say that the tongue, lips, and mouth mentioned in Romans 3 can correlate to the fingers we text with. To use the language of the passage, deception, venom, curses, and bitterness permeate the texts and images on our phones. We can use our phones to hurt others, intentionally and unintentionally. In summary, humanity is a harsh species.

Perhaps you've experienced something similar to my example of Trevor and Nathan. What makes interactions like the above so difficult is the possibility of innocence. Maybe your friend posted an update or sent a photo with good intentions. Maybe the text—"Miss you, man!"—is sincere. But maybe it isn't, and that's what makes life through our devices so difficult. This is what makes me shout *Thank you, Jesus!* in my heart. Why? In contrast to our sinful harshness and mistreatment of one another, Jesus was (and is) a perfect friend.

Jesus both defined and embodied the truest picture of friendship when he died out of love for sinners like you and me. He said it best: "Greater love has no one than this, that someone lay down his life for his friends" (John 15:13). Not only was Jesus the perfect example of true, godly friendship, but he lived out this friendship while receiving hatred and harshness from the world, and even betrayal from his disciples. This means Jesus is not simply a good example of friendship; he's also perfectly able to empathize with us when we experience harshness and rejection from the world (even from our friends). And because he died, he paid the price for the harshness we inflict on others and the harshness inflicted on us.

Without his grace, we wouldn't stand a chance.

More Challenges

In addition to the previous example, there are other interactions that are easy to misinterpret. Perhaps it's a picture of three of your friends with the caption, *hanging out with my besties*, knowing you were not included.

Then there are outright sinful actions through what's written or posted. This could be people trying to stir the pot about religious or political statements by mocking others who believe certain things. Then there are those who post images that are lustful or borderline pornographic. These actions are not loving our neighbors as Jesus called us to.

We must search our own hearts as we interact with others through our devices. At the same time, we need to be prepared for the fact that the people we interact with might simply act harshly and sinfully toward us. While we seek to foster humility and love through social media, we must realize that people are not naturally bent toward kindness.

Harshness will continue to be a part of life in this fallen world, whether it's through our devices or not, so we need to be prepared for that. Sometimes Christians can fall into the trap of coming up with a solution to our social media woes apart from Christ. We may think that abstaining from social media altogether or limiting screen time will resolve the relational tension we feel through various platforms. While times of abstaining from or limiting screen time can be appropriate and called for by some Christians, they don't totally solve the problem of other people's harshness. Plus, these preventative measures do not necessarily point us to Jesus, even though they may be necessary measures for some believers.

This may seem like a pessimistic outlook on life, but I think many would make that claim about Romans 3. You see, being honest about humanity doesn't mean fostering a heart of negativity or cynicism. Christians should have a truthful worldview about humanity. By God's grace, Christians believe that all people—believers and unbelievers—are capable of good. Not good that earns salvation, but acts of kindness and charity toward one another. At the same time, all people—believers and unbelievers—are capable of horrible, unspeakable acts of evil.

Despairing over this evil isn't the answer. Being naïve or oblivious isn't helpful either. It's important to keep a proper theology of the harshness of humanity before us as we enter the world. And it's even more important to see the grace and compassion Jesus had toward harsh people like you and me. Without a doubt, there are times Jesus spoke strong words to people who needed a rebuke, but he also showed grace, mercy, and compassion to those who didn't deserve it. Can you think of a way to show compassion through social media or text? Maybe you're dealing with a specific scenario right now that's difficult. Could you use this as a means of showing the compassion of Jesus to another person?

Jesus experienced perfected love in the Trinity. He tasted perfect unity with the Father and Spirit, but he chose to dwell in the midst of a harsh world. Out of love for his Father, he heard harsh words from mouths he created. He felt harsh actions. Jesus felt what you're feeling, and he's alongside you in whatever harshness you're dealing with today.

Practice

Sadness and social media go hand-in-hand. There's really no way to avoid this. That said, what follows is a practice that may assist you. You see, so often people scroll through social media and feel worse afterward, but they rarely stop to ask why.

Here's what I want you to do.

Sit down for some social media journaling sessions. You don't need to do this every time you get on social media, but plan to have these sessions once a day or a few times per week. Open your notes app or, even better, write on actual paper. A bullet journal or pocket-sized notebook will work just fine.

When you scroll across a post that makes you feel sad, discouraged, angry, or any negative thought, immediately pause on that post. Instead of scrolling to the next image to try and relieve, distract from, or forget your negative feelings, sit with them for a bit. Ask God to show you what might be going on in your heart and mind; pray that he would help you see your heart clearly. Reflect on why you're feeling the way you are by asking questions like these:

- What am I feeling right now?
- Why am I feeling this way?
- Am I justified in feeling this way?
- Was I excluded from something?
- Was the post explicitly sinful?
- Was it specifically aimed at/addressed to me?

There are plenty of other questions you could ask, but these should get you started on reflecting. So often, when we come across images or posts that feed us with negative feelings, we bury them with other images. Then, we begin to feel terrible without really knowing why.

Having these journaling sessions should help you pause and reflect. If you're justified in your feelings, there should be some vindication in that. If you're not, you should repent of those feelings and know that Jesus forgives you. The point of this journal is to foster reflection on what you're experiencing, but it's also to foster prayer (note the previous chapter's practice section). The journal should clarify a lot of what you're feeling, which should help you know what to pray for and how to pray more specifically. If you do this consistently, you can reflect over time and potentially notice patterns and temptations you may be susceptible to.

If you don't have much time and don't like to journal, keep it very simple. If you do like to journal and have more of an artistic bent, take your time and lean into the bullet journal method. Just be sure to talk to God and turn these thoughts into prayers. He's listening.

SONG

"Broken Heart" by Andy Gullahorn

DAY 4: OTHERS' HARM

"You have heard that it was said, 'You shall not commit adultery.' But I say to you that everyone who looks at a woman with lustful intent has already committed adultery with her in his heart." (Matthew 5:27–28)

QUESTION

Plucking out eyes and chopping off hands. No, I'm not talking about a scene in a horror movie. Yes, I am trying to get your attention. I'm pretty sure Jesus was as well when he continued his teachings on the topic of lust by saying,

> "If your right eye causes you to sin, tear it out and throw it away. For it is better that you lose one of your members than that your whole body be thrown into hell. And if your right hand causes you to sin, cut it off and throw it away. For it is better that you lose one of your members than that your whole body go into hell." (Matthew 5:29–30)

It needs to shock us. Jesus means business. Have you given much thought to this passage? I think sometimes our familiarity with these verses decreases the shocking nature of what's being said.

Jesus is known for being a good teacher. Of course, we know Jesus isn't simply using this example for shock value. He is trying to get us to grasp the severity of lust. Maybe we could say that the severity of this example illustrates the severity of Jesus's love for us.

Scripture

Imagine the crowds of everyday people—men, women, children, business owners, and bondservants—pressing in to hear Jesus deliver the Sermon on the Mount (Matthew 5–7). Maybe it was hot outside as people huddled under the blazing sun, trying to cool off but determined to stay and hear this teacher. Maybe some were ill and injured, but they came anyway because of the things they'd heard about Jesus. I wonder what they expected to hear. How many of them saw Jesus just as a teacher? How many of them knew he was the Savior they so desperately needed?

While speaking the very words of God to this great crowd of listeners, Jesus talks about lust as something very serious. We know it's serious because of the shocking illustration he uses, but also because he warns about the fires of hell as a consequence of sin (verse 30). Jesus isn't guilt-tripping people over their lust, simply trying to make them feel condemned or scared enough to behave themselves. He is helping them grasp the seriousness of their sin and their deep and desperate need of a Savior. He is pointing beyond a mere behavior problem to a heart problem.

You see, people actually thought they were obeying the commandment to not commit adultery because they weren't participating in the actual, physical act of adultery. But Jesus prompts them to think not just about their actions, but about their *heart and mind* (verse 28). He graciously points out their misunderstanding of the depth of sin.

In highlighting their heart's intent, Jesus is trying to guard them from harm. This is part of why God gives us commands.

He gives us commands because they reveal his character, and obeying them are a way we can express our love for him. But he also gives us commands to protect us from harming ourselves. His commands are given from a heart of love, not restrictiveness or hate. When we feed lustful desires in our hearts, we do great harm to ourselves and one another.

Story

While writing this chapter, I received an email from a youth worker several states away. This youth worker asked me for help with an issue that continues to increase in prevalence. Based on the verses listed above, you can probably guess that the issue I'm referring to is pornography.

It's an email that's all too familiar. The youth worker contacts me, exchanges small talk at the beginning, and then gets to the main issue: one of their students is struggling with porn. Sometimes a student has been struggling for months. Other times its years before anyone discovers this secret sin. There are times when a student comes to them asking for help and then there are times when a student has been caught and is forced to get help.

The email I received this week was slightly different from previous emails. How so? It was a young girl who was looking at porn. The youth worker who reached out to me was female and the student who was struggling was female. When I first mentioned the email, did you assume the struggling student was a boy? It is a common misconception that porn and lust are primarily male struggles, but it's important we recognize these sins affect both genders.

Many years ago, a woman named Helen Thorne was working for a publisher. She had a deadline approaching for an article, but had no idea what she was going to write about. As the deadline grew closer, she decided to write about women and their struggles with lust, fantasy, and pornography. She hurriedly wrote the article, and it was soon posted on the publisher's website.

Although Helen knew this was a sensitive and vulnerable article, she didn't give much thought to it when it went live online. She went to lunch, and when she came back to the office her colleague came to her with some news. Helen's article had received an unusually high amount of traffic. Due to this high volume of traffic, her colleague encouraged her to write a book on the same subject. After conversation, convincing, and prayer, Helen wrote *Purity Is Possible*. In it, she detailed her own struggles and spoke of the hope Jesus gives.[1]

Helen displayed true courage by sharing her story, and by writing about something few women had written on at the time her article was posted. Praise God she did! Countless women have been ministered to because of Helen's bravery.

For the longest time, the church had seen lust and pornography as male problems. But, as Helen states, "One in three visitors to porn sites are female. . . . Even more of us are using erotica. We tend not to call it that—it sounds better to refer to it as 'romance.'"[2] Similar to Jesus talking about lust in the Sermon on the Mount, people don't think they have a problem. They downplay their struggle.

The Harm of Pornography

I've spent most of this chapter talking about women and pornography because it's very typical to exclusively address guys when discussing this issue. It's important to highlight women and tell them they are not alone. That said, I don't want to be dismissive of guys who struggle. The point is that neither men nor women are immune to the temptations of lust, fantasy, and porn. Through all of this, I want to guard from heaping guilt and shame on anyone who is struggling. This is a very sensitive issue. The good news is this: Jesus's saving power is far greater than this sin.

If you struggle with lust, fantasy, porn, or any sin struggle in this specific area, please know there is hope and forgiveness in Jesus Christ. It's important for us to discuss the harm this sin causes both to you and to others, but we must also remember that Jesus is more powerful than this sin.

The harms caused by lust and porn are vast and are not to be taken lightly. It's tempting to think that lust and porn are just thoughts or habits that we practice, but in reality, they are shaping our thought patterns and our heart's desires. You may even be comfortable viewing images of guys or girls because they aren't explicitly pornographic, but are they lustful? What is going on at a heart level when you look at these images?

These images affect the real people around us because they create a false vision of what love is. Instead of love being outward facing, toward other people, it becomes about us getting what we want. It becomes self-serving. Instead of seeing people as beloved image bearers of God (even fellow Christians, who are our brothers and sisters in Christ), we see them as objects to fulfill our desires and meet our needs. This hurts them and us. Think of the young girls who long to find the man of their dreams, only to get married and discover he has a porn addiction. His devotion to these images makes her feel unloved. Or consider a woman who struggles to find a man attractive because he doesn't measure up to the images she's fed herself through Instagram. Real men and women are being harmed by feeding lustful desires.

Lust and porn also feed our self-centeredness. When you view porn or entertain lustful thoughts, what are those images and thoughts ultimately about? You. This makes it harder to engage in real life because real life does not revolve around us like the people in our lustful fantasies do. This selfishness and lack of real love for real people is the opposite of what Christ is like.

Like Jesus's audience, which was made up of people who misunderstood the depth and dangers of sexual sin, many teenagers today are possibly harming themselves without knowing it. While you consider the dangers of the images you look at, let us also consider the images that you post.

How Are You Posting?

Are you posting content with the subtle desire for others to lust after you? The stance, the angle, the filters, the facial expression—much of these often seem to have been shaped by the porn industry and its objectification of people. Is this true of the images you post?

Guys, are you posting pictures of yourself without a shirt on? Girls, are you posting pictures of yourself in revealing attire? Are your posts trying to emphasize certain body parts? Is the camera positioned in such a way as to highlight yourself in a lustful manner? These questions are for girls and guys—this sin isn't isolated to either gender.

Let me also give a caution about a behavior that may seem completely innocent. How much time are you spending staring at people's pictures? Before social media, you didn't have easy access to a classmate's picture. You could see their photo in the school yearbook, or, if you kind of liked them, you would give them a school picture to keep in their wallet.

Now, however, you post a picture on Instagram and have no idea how many people are looking at it—staring at it with lustful intent. While you cannot control how people view your picture through social media, you can, by God's grace, control how you look at others' pictures. Do you find yourself lustfully staring at others? Do you fail to see them as brothers or sisters, and instead see them as bodies or objects to fulfill your desires? Ask God to search your heart over this matter. You should also ask yourself if you're idolizing an individual. If you find yourself drawn to a specific person and constantly seeking their posts, this infatuation shouldn't be taken lightly.

As I said, I do not want to shame you. It is important to get specific in order to help you grow, to help you search your heart and not only consider *what* you're viewing or posting but *how* you're viewing it. What is your heart's desire as you scroll through someone's pictures? Are you feeding your heart in an unhealthy manner?

You may think the images you look at or post are PG or PG-13, so it's "no big deal." Or you may think that no one gets hurt when you look at a pornographic image, so it's harmless. Jesus, however, is warning you. God's Word says you are hurting yourself, you are hurting others, and, ultimately, you hurt the Son of God by nailing him to a cross, if you are his child.

If you are a Christian, know that Jesus died a bloody death on the cross because he loved you. Although it was an agony beyond our imagining, he gladly died out of love for his Father's will and out of love for you. He also knows that this sin will never bring you the real, full, and eternal satisfaction that it promises. Only Jesus can offer that—and he is true to his Word. Satan wants to plague you with guilt for your sin of lust, but Jesus wants you to know that your guilt and shame were paid in full. If you believe this in your heart, let it shape what and how you view and post on social media.

Practice

One of the most important aspects of this devotional is the Alongsider. Whoever you have picked for your Alongsider will be absolutely vital for this chapter. The Christian life was meant to be lived in community. You cannot fight the good fight of faith without friends.

This may be the most difficult practice section in this book, but I want you to talk to your Alongsider about issues related to lust. By God's grace, some people don't struggle as much in this area as others, but it's likely a struggle in some way for anyone on social media. Whether it was an accidental sighting of an inappropriate image, or an intentional search, it's important to talk with someone about your relationship to lust and/or pornography.

The apostle Paul gives this warning: "Let anyone who thinks that he stands take heed lest he fall" (1 Corinthians 10:12). If you don't struggle at all in this area, it is still important to remain on guard and transparent with other believers. Give thanks to God and share how the struggle isn't as strong for you, but heed Paul's warning about thinking you're above this struggle.

Let me also give this last encouragement. If your Alongsider is the same age as you, it may be important to reach out to someone older—a mentor, pastor, youth worker, coach, or teacher—especially if you are, or recently have been, viewing pornography on a regular basis. Satan wants you to keep this sin in the dark because it grows in the dark. Shine a light on it by sharing it with a trusted older Christian and know that Christ offers both the forgiveness and joy that this sin can never bring you.

SONG

"Covenant Eyes" by Trip Lee and Derek Minor

THE WEEKEND CONVERSATION

1. Which day stuck out to you the most and why?
   - ❐ OTHERS HAVE
   - ❐ OTHERS' HAPPINESS
   - ❐ OTHERS' HARSHNESS
   - ❐ OTHERS' HARM

2. Can you think of a specific social media moment from this past week that reveals some of the ways you struggle?

3. Which of the heart issues that we dug into this week—FOMO, envy, harshness, lust—most resonates with you?

4. Can you think of a specific social media moment from this past week which showed how you have begun to change some of your thinking or habits around these social media struggles?

5. Which of the Practices did you enjoy most? Which helped you to connect with Jesus?

6. Which song and/or lyric did you most resonate with? Why?

7. How can your Alongsider be praying for you?

WEEK 3

DAY 1: OUR WORSHIP

God is our refuge and strength, a very present help in trouble. Therefore we will not fear. (Psalm 46:1–2a)

Question

What are you afraid of? What scares you? Creepy, crawly spiders? The unknown? Social rejection from friends or family? The murky darkness beneath you when you're swimming in the ocean? Failing grades? Some of us might not like to admit we're afraid, but every human is fearful of something. Some of our fears are completely irrational, but some are very real.

Here's a follow-up: What do you do with your fears? Where do you go when you experience fear? How do you deal with the things that scare you? Do you distract yourself from them? Talk yourself out of fear? Or do you take them to the Lord in prayer? Do you let God's Word speak into your fears?

Scripture

I'm not sure if your church has a children's message on Sunday mornings, but mine does. I know people have different opinions about children's messages, but here's one helpful thing about them—they often have one basic truth. The pastor often gives a clear, simple message that's accessible to young listeners. If I gave a children's message on Psalm 46, the basic truth would be this—God is really strong.

We can look all over Scripture to see God's strength. We see it at the very beginning of creation, at the very end with his return, and everywhere in between. We refer to God's strength as his omnipotence. Psalm 46 is a great psalm to highlight this attribute.

This psalm compares God to a fortress. Fortress! That word just has such power to it. I picture a heavy stone structure, broad and tall, that's impenetrable from any attack of an enemy. Well, this is our great God. He's a fortress that protects us from the horrific, valid fears of a broken world.

Story

In 2015, CNN released a documentary entitled *#Being 13: Inside the Secret World of Teens.*[1] The description reads, "More than 200 eighth graders from across the country allowed their social media feeds to be studied by child development experts who partnered with CNN." What they found was pretty shocking at the time, but is now fairly common knowledge. Below are two quotes from the documentary:

- "I would rather not eat for a week than get my phone taken away. It's really bad. . . . I literally feel like I'm going to die."—Gia
- "When I get my phone taken away, I feel kind of naked. . . . I do feel kind of empty without my phone."—Kyla

Throughout the course of the documentary, the teenagers, parents, sociologists, and clinical psychologists used a word that has become commonplace when talking about smartphones. That word? *Addiction.* Over the next few chapters, we're going to look at the addictive nature of social media. Addiction is such a major factor in this entire discussion, and is such a delicate and confusing topic, so it's important to spend some time reflecting on it.

It's also vital to know that we're going to be looking at addiction through the lens of Scripture. Let me state the obvious: I am not a medical professional. There is so much nuance and depth to the topic of addiction, so please know these chapters do not intend to diagnose or address anything medically. However, since addiction is such a pervasive aspect of this conversation, it would be a mistake to omit it from a book about social media.

Worship vs. Addiction

It's been said that addiction is a worship disorder.[2] In reality, we might not have a diagnosable addiction to our phones, but many of us worship our devices in ways that mirror addiction. Some of our social media practices may fall short of true addiction, but we look to them as a false god. We expect them to bring the fulfillment, joy, and deliverance that only God can.

One way to think about this discussion is to think about what we mean when we refer to God as our refuge. We may not use the word *refuge* that often, and it may seem like a strange word to bring up in a discussion on worship and addiction, but there are parallels.

A refuge is a place of security and safety. A place of comfort. A place we long for. A refuge is a place for weary hearts. You see, refuge implies danger. Think of it like a kid huddled in a blanket fort during a thunderstorm, knees tucked into his chest, hiding away from the frightening rain and thunder. A refuge isn't a place we run to when things are going fine; it's a place we long for when we're afraid. This is one reason why the psalmist uses the image of a fortress—it's a place of protection from danger, suffering, evil, sadness, and pain.

Thus, a refuge is something our hearts desire in a fallen world. You and I, and the rest of humanity for that matter, know that this world is broken. Our hearts know that this world doesn't work in the way that it should. We know there is real hurt, danger, fear, and pain. A natural response to this is a desire for comfort, peace, and security.

Let's apply this to our phones and social media usage. How often do you look to these things as a refuge? Imagine walking into a room filled with people. People are milling around, talking in groups. Everybody else looks like they fit in. When all the faces in the room are unfamiliar, you reach for your phone. This comes from the discomfort of unfamiliarity and the resulting desire for refuge and safety. Or imagine that you've had a long day of school. You got a bad grade on an important exam. You and your friend had a miscommunication that caused a bad fallout and now you're barely talking. Or maybe you're just tired from a busy day of classes and extracurriculars. You're stressed out. So you pull your phone out and begin to scroll. You're looking for comfort and peace . . . refuge.

It's not always *wrong* to pull your phone out and scroll. At the same time, it's not always *okay*. Could it be that at least half the time you pick up your phone, it comes from a desire for refuge? What if a percentage of your social media usage comes from a place of addiction or something similar to an addiction?

It's probably safe to say that a significant portion of the time we check our phones comes from an unhealthy place in our hearts. We need to be wise and humble enough to admit that some of the time our social media habits come from a place of false worship—looking to phones or social media to meet our deepest need for connection, comfort, safety, and affection. To say it another way, it would be foolish to assume that scrolling is void of any idolatry. This addiction bears fruit in the ways we seek refuge in things other than God.

The psalmist reminds us that God is our refuge *in the midst of* trouble. He's not saying that God removes all trouble from our lives, but that he's with us in it. He is the only true safe place his children can run to for security. This psalm, however, also reminds us that we will have a tendency to look elsewhere for comfort and security.

Our phones are often able to distract us temporarily, but they don't solve the root fear or struggle we're facing. For example, if you're humiliated by someone at school, you could run to your phone to distract yourself or to retaliate by posting something unkind about them. Or, you could run to God and pour out your pain through prayer or by reading the Psalms. Will this immediately change your situation? No, but it will give you an opportunity to be reminded that he sees you with dignity and worth because he made you in his image. Over time, you can be reminded that people's words may be painful, but they do not define who you are. Running to God can also shape your heart and help you refrain from retaliating in sinful anger.

We live in a world of constant trouble; the psalm goes on to detail those troubles: "... the earth gives way ... the mountains [are] moved into the heart of the sea . . . its waters roar and foam ..." (verses 2–3). The details of the psalm are pretty bleak. Picture any scene from an apocalyptic movie and that's what this psalm describes. Although the psalmist tells us that God is our help in the midst of this worst-case scenario, we know our sinful hearts don't always believe that.

Broken people will look to broken places for security. Even good things can be turned to idols when we expect them to be our refuge. The fears and troubles of this world often reveal the idols of our heart. Sadly, we can profess to believe one thing, but pain shows us otherwise. As we begin to analyze our addictive tendencies through social media, it's important to reflect on this notion of refuge. Are you using your device as a distraction from pain or as a place you run to in order to forget about your fears? By God's grace, begin to ask him to help you see him as the refuge he truly is.

As clichéd as this may sound, run to Jesus for refuge. How do you do that? Talk to Jesus. Tell him what you're afraid of and what you're feeling. Talk out loud to Jesus. Seriously, say one thing you're afraid of right now. You can be completely honest with him. He already knows. He won't be shocked or surprised by your fears and needs. How else do you run to Jesus? Open the Bible. Read it. Pray over it. Those words are Jesus speaking to you personally.

Practice

Sometimes addictions and idols are so sneaky that we hardly notice them day to day. Think of how many times you pick up your phone without even thinking about it. You swipe the screen and blue light shines on your face. You're met by multicolored apps and endless things to search for and videos to watch. You can do all this without really thinking about it. If you're going to fight an idol, though, you need to first identify it. We've just talked about being cautious about picking up your phone, but in this practice, I am asking you to pick it up . . . at least at the beginning.

Most phones tell you how often you pick up your device. I want you to pick up your device and look at what your current average is. Then, try to decrease your average over this next week.

You can get as creative as you want. You can make a colorful chart to document how you spend your time apart from your phone. You can log your average screen time on a calendar in your room. Use your talents and gifts to make this a fun practice, but the main goal is to start picking up your phone less.

You see, we often pick up our phones in a thoughtless way. We just reach for them reflexively. I hope this practice will begin to reveal the times you reach for your device. I hope you not only become more aware of the times you reach for your device, but also that you become aware of the times you *desire* your phone. I don't want this practice to become a means to self-righteousness, or an exercise in mere willpower, but I do want it to create an awareness.

Also, if you feel up to it, consider starting a few good habits. Since you'll be attempting to stop picking up your phone, replace that desire with some good practices. Maybe as you notice the desire to pick up your phone, you say a short prayer: "God, help me seek you as my true refuge." Maybe you could jot a verse of Scripture down and read that when you desire to pick up your phone. Journal, do a chore (I tried to sneak that in), go for a short walk, read a book, have a conversation with your parents—something other than what your device may offer.

SONG

"His Mercy Is More" by Matt Boswell and Matt Papa

DAY 2: OUR SIN

For I do not understand my own actions. For I do not do what I want, but I do the very thing I hate. . . . For I have the desire to do what is right, but not the ability to carry it out. For I do not do the good I want, but the evil I do not want is what I keep on doing. (Romans 7:15, 18b–19)

Question

You storm upstairs and slam the door, angry about your parents' rules that seem so unfair. You spoke harsh words to them. Maybe you said "I hate you" in your frustration. Maybe you meant it in the moment, but after a while you feel the creeping pangs of regret. This is the fourth time this month you've blown up at your parents and yelled at them. *Why do I keep doing this? I regret getting angry, promise to do better, and then after a while I do it again! What is wrong with me?*

Can you relate to this? It may not be yelling at your parents, but do you ever get frustrated at yourself for some behavior, attitude, or habit you can't seem to shake? I think *yes* is a pretty safe assumption. Life in this fallen world is often frustrating, and it's common to have that frustration turned on ourselves. What do you get frustrated about?

If you're frustrated that you're not fast enough or aren't as gifted as someone in a specific way, that's a different category of frustration. Being gifted differently from someone else might not always be fun, but it's not a moral problem. It's not wrong to be a slow runner or just an okay singer. However, if you're frustrated over doing things you shouldn't be doing, or not doing things you should do, that's understandable. Maybe it's even appropriate. That's what Paul communicates in the above verses. It is frustrating when we feel stuck in our sin.

Scripture

This may sound strange, but, to me, what the apostle Paul says in Romans is encouraging. I am not saying that "doing evil" is an encouragement. I don't take joy in my inability to carry out what is good. I'm encouraged because I read those verses and think, *Thank goodness I'm not the only one!* Paul struggled with sin the same way I do.

Paul wanted to do good, but he did evil. Paul didn't want to do evil, but he did. Paul was a deeply flawed person . . . and so am I. So are you. We do the things we don't want to do and don't do the things we should.

Now, I'm skipping ahead, but I don't want to leave us feeling hopeless. Paul ends this chapter feeling hopeless but begins chapter 8 with these words: "There is therefore now no condemnation for those who are in Christ Jesus" (Romans 8:1). While it's encouraging to know we're not alone in our struggle, it's more encouraging to know that Jesus rescues strugglers. We'll continue to hear of the hope of the gospel, but right now we need to continue to think about the struggle of sin.

Story

Before I came on staff with Reformed Youth Ministries, I attended one of their summer youth conferences with my students. During the day, there was an elective for youth leaders. The leader of this class said something like this, "All of you [youth leaders] need to be on Facebook, because that's where all your students are." We can laugh at this statement now because of how dated it seems, but at the time it was a relevant suggestion.

The speaker made this statement when Facebook was gaining popularity and when most adults weren't on it. This was long before Twitter and Instagram. Facebook was about the only social media platform available, and students were all over it. So, I followed this leader's advice and made an account.

After the conference, I remember getting to the office most days and opening Facebook on my computer. I would do some work and then log back on to see what my students were up to. Checking Facebook became part of my job description. It was a task in my daily routine. Before long, however, I noticed the urge to check it more, to log on when I was bored. I also noticed that it felt like I couldn't resist checking Facebook. It was compulsive. That familiar blue logo popped up on my screen throughout the day as I scrolled, liked, and checked new statuses. My time on Facebook extended beyond my office into my home. It went beyond my job description.

I started to have subtle concerns about my behavior with Facebook. I wondered, *What is wrong with me? Why am I always checking Facebook? Do I have a problem?* The lack of control Paul expresses above seemed to describe my concerns about my social media habits.

I'm not sure how long this went on, but, to my relief, I started to hear rumblings about others who had this problem. More and more, people began writing about similar problems of too much screen time, checking Facebook repeatedly throughout the day. Then, the word *addiction* popped up in the conversation. At first, people scoffed at anyone attaching the word *addiction* to their social media usage. Reality, however, has set in for those who were dismissive of the addictive nature of social media.

Are You Addicted?

If you have a social media platform, I assume you've experienced something similar to my struggles with Facebook. If not, that's great. Research, however, seems to point to the reality that many of you reading this are either in a category classified as addicted or are somewhere close to that.[1]

Everyone reading this is different. We have different desires and disciplines. We have different upbringings. Our home environments are unique. The variables that factor into addictions are vast, to say the least. So, I want you to be honest in your self-evaluation. If you're reading this book, chances are that you notice tendencies of concern. Therefore, the more honest you are, the more helpful this book will be. Let's return to these words from Paul.

We could fill an entire book detailing all that Paul says in this section of Romans, but the big picture is a description of our sin nature: "Now if I do what I do not want, it is no longer I who do it, but sin that dwells within me" (7:20). The truth is, some of our addictive tendencies are simply sin. It's challenging to separate our sin nature from our identity, which often makes the intertwined nature of sin and addictions difficult to understand.

Think back to the previous chapter. We saw how our desires for escape/refuge are connected to our addictive tendencies. As sinners we can, and often do, turn to false gods to give us what only the true God can. One definition of sin is "the fundamental unbelief, distrust and rejection of God and *human displacement of God as the center of reality*" (emphasis added).[2]

As sinners, we seek to displace God from the center of reality. God is perfectly pure and holy, but we seek to displace him and put something else there. I don't know what it was about Facebook, but it became something that filled in the cracks of my day. In very real ways, I had lost control of my body and my sin was taking over. This doesn't take responsibility away from me, though. I'm not saying I'm innocent.

Facebook would offer me an escape. Sometimes it was an escape from boredom. Sometimes it was an escape from responsibility. There were times it was an escape to something humorous—maybe a funny picture, video, or post. Again, sometimes this was innocent, but sometimes this came from places of sin in my heart—laziness, lust, control, escape. The more subtle, fun aspects of Facebook were feeding idols of comfort, ease, and pleasure. And, because of the habitual nature of social media, I began forming addictive tendencies in my use of Facebook. Ask yourself this: Is there anything I am using to escape difficulty, boredom, or discomfort? What do I spend most of my days looking at or seeking out? When do I most often turn to my phone and social media?

As you begin to evaluate your social media habits, I want to give you three helpful categories for reflection:

1. **Relax:** Some of your scrolling is simply light-hearted fun that you have freedom to enjoy. If this is the case, relax. Be cautious of your sin nature, but don't feel guilt over enjoying some of the better aspects of social media.
2. **Refuse:** Some of your scrolling is coming from places of sinful idolatry in your heart. Maybe you check social media too often to see if you've received more likes on a photo. It's not the interest in likes that's the problem, but have you considered that people's approval may be an idol for you? If this is true, refuse to indulge your temptations to check social media too much through the power the Spirit gives you. Take your sin to Jesus and ask for strength to fight sin and believe in the forgiveness he offers.
3. **Request:** Some of you may be in a place where you feel powerless over the dominance your device has over you. You feel like it's impossible for you to have any control over it. If this is you, cry out to God for deliverance, and request help from a trusted adult in your life—maybe this is your Alongsider.

There are times when our sin is to blame for our addictive tendencies, but our phones are partly to blame as well. While we don't overlook our own sin, we must acknowledge the addictive aspects that are hardwired into our devices that make it harder to use them with wisdom and self-control—and that's what we'll look at in the next chapter.

Practice

At the risk of sounding like a broken record, it's not always easy to figure out if something is sinful or not. The human heart is a confusing thing. If you look at the above three categories and are unsure of whether you should relax, refuse, or request, below are some good diagnostic questions to help you think a bit more.

- Is your phone the first thing you reach for in morning?
- Do you sleep with your phone?
- Are you rarely without your phone?
- Do you feel like it would be impossible to be without your phone for an hour or a few hours?
- Can you ever go to the bathroom without your phone?
- Do you always have to have it in sight?
- Can you go a day without your phone? Does that sound impossible?
- Are most of your notifications for social media turned on? Do you feel like you could turn all (or some) of your notifications off?
- When you post something, how quickly and how often do you check for reactions to your post? Do you just sit there and refresh?
- How often do you turn your phone's airplane mode on or off?
- How frequently do you switch from one app to another and then back again?

These aren't all the questions you could ask yourself, but they are a helpful starting point. If you read through this list quickly, I would encourage you to go back and take your time answering them. Take out a sheet of paper and write out your answers. Or, go back to that journal from other practices. Spend some time reflecting. Most importantly, pray through that list and ask God to give you wisdom to clearly access your own heart. Wherever you fall, remember that Jesus is alongside his children. He is ready to forgive us and help us when we fail.

SONG

"One Sixteen" by Trip Lee

DAY 3: OUR TECHNOLOGY

Little children, keep yourselves from idols. (1 John 5:21)

Question

Have you ever heard someone say that your heart is an idol factory? This phrase comes from a famous theologian named John Calvin. While Calvin was commenting on the sinful nature of our hearts, this truth he articulated actually comes from the Bible.

Have you given much thought to your idols? When you're trying to fall asleep at night, what fills your mind? For that cute boy to finally ask you out? What do you daydream about? Winning a championship game and getting that athletic scholarship to college? What do you spend your time working on, pursuing, or practicing? Studying? Extracurriculars? What do you spend most of your money on? Books, food, makeup, tech? What does your internet search history say about what you are most interested in? The answers to these questions can help you discover what you love most and, therefore, what might be an idol in your life.

As you reflect on those questions and come up with an answer, you may think, *This can't be my idol because it's not even something bad.* This, however, is what's so tricky about our idols. As we said earlier, often our idols are actually good things that we try to put in the place of God. We make them ultimate things.

Scripture

The verse for this chapter is almost comical. I'm not saying that John is being lighthearted or that we should take idolatry lightly. There's nothing funny about idol worship.

When I say the verse is comical, it's because of its context. The verse seems totally out of place! If you read the entire chapter of 1 John 5, verse 21 comes out of nowhere. You get whiplash because you weren't even ready for it. It's a gut punch.

A closer reading reveals that this verse isn't as out of left field as we may have thought. John is telling us that we have understanding of who the true God is (verse 20), and part of our knowledge and understanding of God will be seen in our fight against idolatry. Therefore, those who call themselves Christians will keep themselves from idols. And, as we will see, our technology serves many of the idols of our heart.

Story

As we've seen so far, technology addiction is a multifaceted, complex issue. For Christians, it is important to address our hearts and get to the root of *why* we do the things we do—it's simply the proper biblical approach. To maintain balance, though, we would be mistaken to assume that technology plays an innocent party in this discussion.

Years ago, I stumbled upon a rather disturbing animated short entitled, *The Super Rope Solution*.[1] The cartoon illustrated the convenience technology offers, but also the unintended consequences and laziness it can enable. As illustrated in the video, convenience can come at a price.

The main character of the cartoon is a lazy man. He lives in a small apartment, sits in an old recliner all day, too lazy to do anything, evidenced by his plump form. He's hungry, but is too lazy to go to the fridge and get something to eat, even though the fridge is a short walk from the recliner he's lounging in. However, he sees a commercial for a rope that can solve this problem. While remaining in his recliner, he can simply pull the rope which opens the refrigerator door and brings the food to him. So he buys the rope. Problem solved.

However, a new problem emerges. He now has trash to deal with, but he's obviously too lazy to get up and throw it away. Well, he sees another advertisement for a new rope that can take away his trash. He buys that rope and simply pulls it when he's done, and it cleans up his meal. Once again, problem solved.

The cartoon depicts him buying numerous ropes to solve his various inconveniences. Before long, his tiny apartment is covered in ropes. They seem to take up every square inch. The man gets to a point where there are too many ropes in his apartment, and he wants to stop buying more of them. But—and this is where the cartoon takes a disturbing twist—the ropes begin to take on a life of their own and make him order more ropes by grabbing his hands and making him pick up the phone. Eventually, he ends up completely tied to his recliner, unable to do anything on his own, seemingly drowning in ropes . . . and that's how it ends. Terrifying, right?

Created for Comfort

As Christians, we know we are created with this innate desire for comfort and ease because we were created for a perfect, sin-free existence with God in the Eden. Although we rebelled, through Jesus, we know we are promised a peaceful existence with God when he returns—that's why we long for rest. This cartoon illustrates how technology can ease so many of life's discomforts and inconveniences. But sometimes our hearts take advantage of this and become enslaved to the ease and apparent abundance technology offers.

It's also true that our idols seem to offer convenience. The obvious example is money. While money can't buy true happiness, it does grant us a lot of temporary happiness. It offers a lot of convenience by allowing us to purchase the next new thing that might make our lives easier or give us something to look forward to. These things can make money an idol of our hearts.

Thinking back to the cartoon, it also illustrates how the addictive nature of our technology is rooted in convenience. Part of the good design of technology is that it often solves problems. Things that were once difficult are now made easy. This ease of use can lead to addictive patterns.

Amazon is an example most of us can relate with. When we want or need something, we don't have to get in our car, wait in traffic, walk through a store, find an item, purchase the item, and then drive back home. We simply touch a button on our phone and someone else does the driving through traffic to arrive at our home—sometimes on the same day. Crazy convenient, right?!

Our technologies are more than just convenient, though. In some cases, they go beyond convenience and take on a life of their own, like the ropes in the cartoon.

The 2020 Netflix documentary *The Social Dilemma* explains how social media platforms make money. Although these platforms are free for users, our attention is the currency we pay. As Tristan Harris, former Google employee and co-founder of The Center for Humane Technology, warns us, "If you aren't paying for the product, then you are the product . . . your attention is the product that is being sold to advertisers."[2] We may think social media is free, but we pay for it through the attention we give to it. This is how we become the product, according to Harris.

As you are probably aware, Amazon keeps up with our purchases and uses that information to suggest other items we might like. It's constantly recommending items we never knew we needed. It reminds us that others with similar purchasing patterns also found "this item interesting." This typically pulls us back in and keeps us purchasing. In this case, the products are searching and finding us. Once again, this is similar to the ropes in *The Super Rope Solution*.

There's a related issue some of you may have experienced. How many times have you been discussing an item or product with your friends through casual conversation, only to find that item appear in your feed later that day? If not the exact item, an item related to the conversation—a conversation you thought was private—with your friends. This isn't simply coincidence. Technology is taking on a life of its own to draw you back in.

Look at Me, Look at Me

Notifications are another way technology keeps drawing us in. They are designed to get you to pick up your phone. Buzzes and beeps easily capture our attention. In fact, Tristan Harris puts it this way: "there's this screen, and then on the opposite side of the screen, there's these thousands of engineers and supercomputers that have goals that are different than your goals, and so, who's going to win in that game? Who's going to win?"[3]

While that reality should sober us, it also should encourage us. I would assume most of you feel guilty—at least a little bit—over how much time you use your device. Research shows that 36 percent of teens say they spend too much time on social media.[4] That stat implies a bit of guilt. As mentioned in the previous chapter, some of that guilt can be connected to our idolatry, but some of the blame can be laid on these platforms. Brilliant engineers and designers have created these technologies to pull you back in. Like *The Super Rope Solution* cartoon, it's not all on you. Yes, our idolatry is to blame, but *technology isn't innocent either*.

We are designed to worship someone or something. Our devices are often one of our biggest idols. That said, these idols are unique because they are designed to attract us in ways other idols don't. Just like the man from the cartoon, our devices can take on a life of their own and overpower us.

As believers, we cannot take addiction lightly because it is strongly correlated with idolatry. If we're looking at our devices hundreds of times a day for hours and hours a day, there's a really good chance that it has become an idol. We feel as though we can't live without the reward we get from looking at our screens. While the addictive tendencies of our devices share some of the blame, our hearts are a big part of the problem. John's warning should sober us. "Keep yourselves from idols" is a caution against the powerful, destructive effect idols inevitably bring about. In short, only God can fill that void, anything else dishonors God and brings harm to ourselves and others.

If you're feeling convicted, or even discouraged, don't forget that John's admonition to "keep yourselves from idols" begins with "dear children." He's addressing those who are loved by the Father. He's reminding them to shun the idols of their heart *because* they are loved with a love that nothing else is capable of giving them.

While we may lack self-control, Jesus didn't. Jesus experienced plenty of temptations around every corner and he resisted every one of them. That righteousness he accomplished has been freely given to those who believe. Jesus has complete control over those who feel out of control. Believe it in your heart. Speak this truth back to yourself. Collapse in his strong arms.

Practice

Since we've determined that some of the blame for addiction belongs to our devices, consider the following ways you can modify your phone to make it less addictive. If you Google "How can I make my phone less addictive?" you will find numerous articles and videos offering ideas. Pick and choose whatever helps you best. Below are some examples:

- Modify your notifications to alert you less. Whatever your current settings are, try and scale them back a little or a lot. Try to completely turn them off for a day or two.

- Change your home screen. Don't put the apps you use the most on your home screen. Make them a little harder to access.
- Some have recommended putting a hairband or rubber band across your phone. This allows you to answer calls easily, but makes the other apps less convenient or, at least, fosters some thoughtfulness when you remove it to access them.
- Delete apps for a day or two. If able, only use the desktop version of the app. This way, you can still keep up with what's going on, but you'll make your device a little less accessible.
- Set up screen limits and actually stick to them. Invite a friend to do this with you.
- Change the colors of your device to grayscale. The lack of color supposedly makes your phone less attractive.
- When you're with friends, choose to keep your phone in your pocket or purse, rather than picking it up throughout your time together. Set your phone to airplane mode if that makes it easier, and if you can do so safely.
- Keep your phone in another room from where you're working. Even if you're not working or doing homework, try to put your phone away for an hour each day.
- Limit the screens. If you tend to scroll on your phone while watching TV, leave it in another room and commit to one screen at a time.
- Have a list of activities to replace your scrolling time. Keep this on hand and easily accessible. Include a mix of fun things and things you need to accomplish. When you're tempted to grab your phone, pick one of these alternative activities instead. See how much more you'll get done and create with this simple swap.

SONG

"He Will Hold Me Fast" by Shane & Shane

DAY 4: OUR DECEIT

The heart is deceitful above all things, and desperately sick; who can understand it? (Jeremiah 17:9)

Question

Have you ever been so sure of something that you adamantly insisted you were right . . . only to find out you were wrong? How did you respond? Do you have a hard time admitting when you're wrong? I think most of us do. I mean, how much fun is it to say, "Hey, you know what? I was wrong and you were right"? That's challenging for most of us.

Pride is a problem for every human heart, and the difficulty of admitting we're wrong is just some of the fruit of that pride.

Scripture

This verse in Jeremiah is one I think about quite often. It doesn't leave much room for misunderstanding. It's a pretty blunt and strong word about the nature of our hearts. *Don't follow your heart. Don't trust your heart. It lies to you all of the time*.

Part of the difficulty of this verse is the fact that we're unable to truly grasp the depth of our heart's problems. The verse itself ends by asking, "Who can understand it?" Our hearts are so poisoned with sin that we're unable to grasp just how fallen they are. To say it this way, we are so sinful that we don't know how sinful we really are.

We might all react differently to the truth of this word, but let me make one suggestion—practice humility. Don't push back. Don't justify. Don't just disagree. Ask God to help you receive it and be humbled by it. Trust me, there's encouragement in this hard verse.

Story

There's a very disturbing scene in the 1999 thriller *The Sixth Sense*.[1] I guess it would be more accurate to say there are several disturbing scenes, which shouldn't be surprising since the protagonist sees dead people. But the specific scene I'm referring to is the discovery of a young girl's death.

Cole Sear (Haley Joel Osment), the one who sees dead people, begins to speak to the recently deceased Kyra Collins (Mishca Barton). After Kyra's terrifying introduction in the film, Cole discovers that she died by poison. As Cole talks more with Kyra, he discovers that it was her mother who poisoned her. Little by little, the mother would slip some poison into her daughter's food. Cole helps to uncover the mystery surrounding Kyra's death and, while the movie doesn't reveal all the details, justice is brought upon the mother for this horrific act. Truly disturbing.

Why do I share this scene from a movie that dates back to 1999? It helps to illustrate an important truth. Did you know you and I are being poisoned? No, I'm not poisoning you and you aren't poisoning me. We are all poisoning *ourselves*.

In the opening verse, we read that our hearts are "deceitful above all things, and desperately sick." I know this verse doesn't sound like the most encouraging thing, but it really is, if you stop to think about why it is in the Bible. God, in his loving grace, wrote this passage to tell us about the fallen nature of our hearts. Our hearts lie to us all the time. God is simply being truthful.

Our hearts are poisoned with sin. Like Kyra from *The Sixth Sense*, we drink the poison of our own hearts each and every day. How do we do that? Well, we tell ourselves stories.

When you look at yourself in the mirror, your heart speaks lies, and you drink them down like truth. Maybe you have a conversation with friends and when you leave them, you think, *None of them like me. Everyone hates me.* You drink the poisonous lie from your heart. Perhaps you didn't make the team you tried so hard to make, so you tell yourself you're worthless. You're not athletic like all those other people on the team, so you drink the poison that tells you, *You don't have any value.*

Maybe some of you come from a divorced family. Some of the lies you listen to say that it's your fault. You drink the poisonous lie of your heart that says, *Your parents would still be together if it weren't for you.* If that's you, I am so sorry. If that's you, please silence that lie by the power of the Holy Spirit—that's something we'll talk about more in a minute.

If you look at pornography, you are feeding on a poison that's destroying you. And the dangers of pornography are fueling the lies of your heart. Maybe those images tell you that you must look a certain way to have value for your girlfriend or boyfriend. It could be that you think you're unlovable and could never find someone, so you're telling yourself that pornography offers you some form of love that's unattainable for you.

Whether or not you're on social media, you have a heart that lies to you. When you wake up in the morning, get ready for school, walk down the halls, all the way to when you fall asleep each night, your heart never stops feeding you lies. But social media often amplifies those lies.

A Different Story

In the 2018 film *Spider-Man: Into the Spider Verse*, the protagonist, Miles Morales (Shameik Moore), is driving to school with his father one morning. There's tension in their conversation because Miles is being transferred to a new school. He doesn't want to go to this new school because it seems elitist, but his dad assures him it's a wise move. As he gets out of the police car (his father is a cop), his dad tells him he loves him. Miles, still frustrated at his father, replies, "I know that. See you Friday."[2]

What follows is one of the best dad-moves in recent cinema history. In front of the crowd of students headed to class, Miles's father bumps the police siren and, over the megaphone, says, "You gotta say 'I love you' back." Even though Miles protests, his father continues to interrupt, asking for the reciprocated, "I love you." It's totally embarrassing to Miles in front of all his classmates, but totally awesome at the same time. It's a hilarious moment.

What you and I need to know is that we have a heavenly Father screaming his love to us through a megaphone. Our true Father is not doing that to embarrass us; he's screaming it to us because the lies of our fallen heart can be very loud. And he screams this truth to us through the life, death, and resurrection of Jesus.

You see, when we've been drinking the poison of our lying hearts for so long, we begin to live by the story of those lies. The lies become reality in our mind. We begin to think they're truth. God, in his lovingly relentless pursuit of us, is screaming: *I love you! I love you! I love you*! Our sin is so powerful, however, that we can miss Jesus.

While there is nothing we can do to *un-earn* the Father's love, we must begin telling ourselves the story of his unfailing love. As God's children, we have to learn to silence the lies of the evil one and the lies of our own hearts, and instead hear the truth of who we are in Jesus.

Hearing Truth

How do we hear and believe truth over the lies? One of the best ways is to feed upon God's Word. Often times Bible reading can seem like a chore because it's viewed as something you have to do, like homework or cleaning your room.

Maybe it helps to see Bible reading as the healing medicine for the poison you drink every day. If it's true that our hearts are lying to us (and it is), then you and I need to be regularly drinking from something that's true. God's Word is that truth.

You see, in and of ourselves, you and I don't have the strength to speak truth back to ourselves. So much of the world buys into positive "self-talk," simply looking in a mirror and reciting some sort of positive mantra to ourselves. While there may be some merit to some of that, we have a much better resource: the eternal Word of God.

The Bible is a supernatural book. It possesses power in and of itself. As I've heard other people say, it's the only book that reads *you*. It tells you more about yourself than you know. Sometimes it can sting, but it's speaking the truth in love. The truth of God's Word is powerful enough to cleanse your heart from poisonous lies.

So pick up God's Word. Drink from it. Feed on it. Live in the light of it. Speak its truth back to your heart as much as you can. It has the power to heal your poisonous heart.

Practice

Throughout my years in youth ministry, I've had so many students ask me where to begin in their Bible reading. It's a good question because the Bible is a big book that can seem intimidating. Below are some recommendations, but I would also encourage you to ask someone you trust to give you guidance.

- **Read**: If reading the Bible isn't a common practice, start small! Seriously, start by reading one verse each day for at least three to five days. The following week, try two verses for three to five days. Slowly progress each week, but also be cautious of pushing yourself too fast. As others have said, a little bit of something is better than a whole lot of nothing.
- **Pray**: Bible reading and prayer go hand-in-hand. Pray the most basic prayers before and after you read. Example: *God, please help me focus and understand your Word.* That's a prayer! It doesn't have to be long or fancy. Then, after you read the

verse: *God, please write your Word on my heart and help me believe it.* You're done! If you want a sample prayer card, check out a resource RYM credited (https://www.rym.org/ministry-tools_1/posts/prayer-cards-for-scripture-reading).

- **Speak**: Think about some of the lies you feed yourself consistently. Write those lies down and share them with your Alongsider. Ask them to help you find verses that speak truth back to those lies. Repeat those verses back to yourself consistently.

SONG

"Be Kind to Yourself" by Andrew Peterson

THE WEEKEND CONVERSATION

1. Which day stuck out to you the most and why?
   - ❒ OUR WORSHIP
   - ❒ OUR SIN
   - ❒ OUR TECHNOLOGY
   - ❒ OUR DECEIT

2. Did anything you learn this week about technology, idolatry, addiction, or the deceit of our hearts surprise you? If so, how?

3. How does it make you feel, knowing that social media platforms are intentionally designed to get you to stay on the platform for as long as possible?

4. What are some of the lies that your heart tells you?

5. How does the gospel challenge those lies?

6. How can your Alongsider be praying for you?

WEEK 4

DAY 1: HEART

The intentions of a man's heart are deep waters.
(Proverbs 20:5a BSB)

Question

Imagine meeting your favorite celebrity—a famous singer, actor, or athlete you've admired for years. You manage to snap a selfie with them, your face beaming the whole time as you try to play it cool. What do you do with that photo? Keep it tucked away in your phone or share it on social media? Maybe you text it to your friends?

I know the example of the celebrity doesn't resonate with everyone. For you, maybe it's a video of you singing in a talent show, making a game-winning shot, or telling a crazy story of something impressive that you've seen or done. Odds are, you'd want to share it. There's a desire we have that wants to share these big moments—but why?

You're probably excited, so you want to share that excitement with others. Human nature often wants to share fun and joyous moments with other humans. There's nothing wrong with that, but is it possible to want to share these things for a wrong reason? Think about that for a minute.

Have you given much thought to why you do the things you do? Do you think much about your motives? *Why did I say that? Why did I laugh at that? Why did I share that? Why did I react this way to that comment?* The short answer is—your heart.

Scripture

The first and greatest commandment is to love the Lord our God with all our heart (Deuteronomy 6:5). Therefore, it's of the utmost importance to think about our heart . . . a lot. If you've noticed, that's something I've tried to get you to do through most of this devotional. If the sinfulness of our heart is a truth repeated throughout Scripture, then we need to spend a great deal of time reflecting on our heart.

This may be the most important chapter in this entire devotional. That's because there's a sense in which our heart is absolutely everything. It dictates the choices we make—both good and bad—and the direction we walk. To quote another Proverb, "Above all else, guard your heart, for everything you do flows from it" (Proverbs 4:23 NIV).

Think about the words "Above all else." In other words, guarding your heart is really important. And "everything you do" comes from your heart. The heart impacts everything in your life. The things you say. The things you do. The things you think. They are all connected to the heart.

We need to think about our desires. Which desires of our heart are good and which desires are sinful? As the above Proverb states, the intentions of our hearts are "deep waters." In essence, it's tricky, confusing, and complicated to dig into the depths of our hearts.

Story

When I was in seminary, I remember one of my professors talking about Twitter. He stood in front of the class and shared some of his struggles with the social media platform. As a seminary professor, author, and pastor in a church, he was somewhat of a public figure. Therefore, he knew he had a certain amount of influence. This meant that his tweets contained a certain amount of weight or power. He shared how often he would have a tweet typed up and ready to share, but he would pause before he sent it. He would ask himself,

Why am I about to send this? Am I doing this to gain popularity and influence? Am I doing this because I worship myself and I want others to worship me? He was being vulnerable about his heart. The entire class joined in on a discussion about our intentions for posting what we post.

This professor was sharing a simple, yet helpful practice. Stopping before you post. Another friend of mine calls this a "prayerful pause." Asking "why" can dig down into our heart's desires and motives. It gets us to consider some of the idols we may be feeding:

- Am I about to tweet this because I want to impress others?
- Am I about to share this because I want people to think I'm important?
- Am I sharing this because I'm in a picture with someone prominent and I want others to know that I got to be around someone on this level?
- Am I doing this because I worship myself and I want others to worship me?
- Am I doing this simply for the rush I get from likes/comments/followers?
- Am I sad/depressed and just want some attention?

Why?

In the last chapter we saw how deceitful our hearts are. Scripture tells us that the human heart is so dark and so deceitful that it can often be difficult for us to understand. The truth is that our own hearts tell so many lies, it can be hard for us to know when we're lying and when we aren't. Proverbs 20:5 is right, "The intentions of [our] heart are deep waters."

Here's another way to think about it. The heart is the center of your identity. If I ask, "Who are you?" how would you answer? You could tell me your name. You could tell me where you live, where you attend school, or the activities you're a part of. You could tell me your accomplishments and the clubs you attend. But apart from what you *do*, who *are* you, really? Deep down. In the heart. Because the heart is the core of your being. Your heart houses your desires and motivates your actions. It reveals what you want and love most. It's the real you.

The Real You

There is no telling how many youth retreats and conferences I've attended in my lifetime. I've gone on youth retreats as a youth leader, chaperone, main speaker, and now I attend them as part of my job. I've witnessed many things on youth trips (some I can't mention in this book), but one thing I know is this, you really get to know people when it's time to eat.

What do I mean? When it's time to eat, you get to see the real person. Most of the time, you can act polite, project a friendly persona to others, and make people think you are a loving person. However, when you get hungry, people often get to meet the real you. The you that gets angry when people cut in line. The you that rushes ahead of people to get to the front of the line. The you that takes extra helpings of food with little to no regard for those behind you.

Now, it's annoying when anyone cuts in line, and we have to eat food to survive, but I think you get my point. When we meet someone, we often project a certain image to them. We act like the person we want others to think we are. But who are we in our hearts?

Who you are on the outside matters, but so does the inside. Who you are at the heart level is your true self. The true you. And the true, heart-level you needs to consider this when you're on social media. *What's the motive of your heart? Why are you about to post that picture, comment, tweet, or video?*

Consider the following examples of underlying heart motives:

- Are you posting that picture because you want other people to compliment you? Is your identity in your image, and therefore you need the daily affirmation of others?
- Are you simply posting because you're bored? You've got nothing else to do, so you're just going to share this to distract yourself from deeper reflection.
- Are you posting that comment to gain attention in some way? Do you long for the attention of others, so you're sharing a "hot take" to get people to notice you?
- Do you pride yourself on being a funny person, so you want that affirmation through a post?
- Are you trying to create a following for yourself? Is this feeding pride in your heart because you think they need to hear from you? Do you think people need your commentary on everything that's happening?
- Do you try to project a spiritual persona, perhaps by posting Bible verses to impress others? Do you often share pictures of yourself having a daily devotion in order to boast?
- Are you sharing some good deed you performed because you want the notoriety? Do you want people to see the good thing you did and praise you?
- Is your post simply bragging? Is it feeding a subtle arrogance?

In the Sermon on the Mount, Jesus says a great deal about our hearts. Much of what he says in chapter 6 cautions us about our outward actions in comparison to our hearts. He begins the chapter by saying, "Beware of practicing your righteousness before other people in order to be seen by them, for then you will have no reward from your Father who is in heaven" (Matthew 6:1).

Jesus obviously isn't saying "don't do good to others." He wants us to serve and love others through good deeds. Our good deeds are not done as a way to earn favor with God; they are to be done out of thanksgiving for what Jesus has done for us. Jesus's warning is found in the words "in order to be seen."

Jesus is saying to do good to other people, but "beware" that you aren't doing these things "in order to be seen by them." And that is Jesus's caution to our own hearts. Our hearts are so fallen that we can do good things for the sole purpose of being seen and worshipped by others. Think of how this temptation manifests itself on social media.

J. C. Ryle says this: "[God] takes no account of the quantity of money we give, or the quantity of words we use: the one thing at which his all-seeing eye looks is the nature of our motives and the state of our hearts."[1]

When it comes to the God of all creation, he sees us at the heart level. We may fool ourselves about why we do the things we do, but we can't fool him. God, in his grace, does give us new eyes to see. Those eyes can search our own hearts. God loves to give wisdom to his children and that wisdom helps us discern why we're posting the things we post. In fact, basic wisdom teaches us to question our own heart. Pride doesn't like to do that.

Most importantly, however, God gives his children a new heart. He takes away our heart of stone and gives us a heart of flesh (Ezekiel 36:26). Our new heart is still poisoned with sin and still has to fight to do what is right, but it's a heart that's growing in Christlikeness. It's a heart that grieves its own sin and the sin that poisons this world. It's a heart that, day-by-day, longs to be at home with Jesus. But, as restless as our hearts may be, they can rest assured that he will carry us home.

Practice

You may already be asking the "why" question about what you post. If you aren't, let me encourage you to start making this more of a practice. The goal is not to be overly introspective, but to honestly examine your heart with God's help. Below are a few creative ways to help you start asking "why":

- Calendar: Create a new event in your calendar entitled WHY? Set it as a reoccurring event that will pop up first thing in the morning, in the afternoon, or at any point of your choosing. Keep it on your calendar for a period of time to keep this question on your mind.
- Reminder: If you use a reminder app, create a WHY? reminder. Have it alert you periodically to help you remember to search your heart.
- Wallpaper: Create a colorful, fun, or bland wallpaper on your phone with the word WHY? Anytime you reach for your phone, you'll see this word and will hopefully remember to think about your heart's motivations. Of course, you'll get familiar with this background and forget, but leave it on your phone for a while anyway.
- Text: Find a group of friends, or your Alongsider, and randomly text the word WHY? to them. Text it periodically throughout the day in a group chat or individual text.
- Call: Here's a funny idea. With the same group of friends, call them and ask, WHY? and then just hang up. Obviously tell them ahead of time, but then just randomly call them. If they don't answer, say "WHY?" into their voicemail and just hang up. Do this for a period of time, then stop for a while . . . and then do it again when they don't expect it.

SONG

"You Already Know" by JJ Heller

DAY 2: LOVE

There is no fear in love, but perfect love casts out fear. For fear has to do with punishment, and whoever fears has not been perfected in love. We love because he first loved us. (1 John 4:18–19)

Question

Have you ever given much thought to getting married? For some of you, the answer is an easy "YES!" You've given a lot of thought to it, and it consumes much of your daydreaming—you've perfected the details, from the perfect white dress and a slick black tuxedo to the first dance song and your favorite live band. For others, maybe you've thought about it a little, but it seems like something far off in the future, not really relevant to you today . . . you've got grades to think about! For others, maybe this is your first time thinking about it. You're welcome.

Therefore, let me say something obvious. If you're a Christian who will get married one day, you need to marry another person of the opposite sex who is secure in Jesus's love. If they are not, then chances are they will look to you to be their ultimate source of love and joy. What a crushing burden that is! The reality is, if both of you are not secure in Jesus's perfect, unfailing love, you won't end up loving each other properly.

Scripture

I think many of us would assume that hate is the opposite of love. That's totally understandable. I mean, if you hate someone, you're actively against them. You're not showing love to them. The characteristics of hate seem to be the antithesis of love.

The above verse, however, seems to tell us that the opposite of love is *fear*. This may sound a little strange, but it makes sense when you recognize that love can be connected to vulnerability. Let me explain.

Have you ever told someone you loved them? I'm not talking about your parents or siblings; I'm talking about someone you really, really liked. How did you feel when you got ready to tell them? Maybe your palms were sweaty and you were shaking a bit. Maybe you were red-faced and fidgety, or you stumbled over your words and felt awkward. Maybe it was hard to look them in the eyes. If you were in the presence of someone you loved, why might you have felt anxious? Saying I love you to a person of the opposite sex is a vulnerable, fearful thing, because they might not respond with, "I love you too." And what would this negative response make you feel about yourself? Unloved? Insecure? Unwanted? Embarrassed? Those are fearful things.

So fear and love are more connected than we might think.

Story

I sincerely think YouTube is one of the greatest recent inventions. I use it almost daily.

I have used YouTube to repair many things in my home (or sometimes make things worse with my attempted repairs). It has helped me tackle many woodworking projects I would never have thought possible. YouTube has been educational in so many ways.

If I'm honest, however, I use it more for mindless escape than anything else. You probably know how easy it is to sit back and let the instant play feature take you to the next video . . . and the next, and the next, until it's been a couple hours or more, your eyes are glazed over and you start to forget what sunlight and fresh air feel like. If I have some free time or time when I just want to chill, I'll often get on YouTube. I can use it for constructive purposes or less constructive purposes—neither of which are inherently wrong. That said, YouTube also has some darker, destructive purposes.

Most people who have visited YouTube are well aware of the horrors of this creation. Just like anything else on the internet, it is filled with pornography and all sorts of vileness. We've already devoted a chapter to reflecting on the harm of pornography, so I want us to go in another direction. There is content on YouTube that is more subtle in its potential wickedness.

My main concern is the way we are failing to show love to others through what we consume on this platform (and others). We may actually be perpetuating an unloving spirit in the world through the content we watch and share online. As the opening verse reads, God loved us first. And this is the reason why we are to love others. I want us to pause and reflect on ways in which we may be less than loving to others through some of our everyday practices on social media.

Some Christians may disagree with some of what I'm about to say. They may say it's more innocent fun than something sinful. Hear me out, though, and allow me to explain my concerns before you dismiss them.

The Funny of Fail

YouTube has plenty of "fail videos," videos depicting people failing at some task. Someone turns on the blender, only to realize that they forgot to put on the lid, and immediately their smoothie goes *SPLAT* . . . all over their shocked face. It could be failing at an athletic feat or a stunt—a runner gets tripped up and falls when they can't clear a hurdle or a skateboarder wipes out, skidding painfully down the half pipe on their knees. It could be something more everyday and basic, like walking down the street and slipping on a patch of ice. Some of these are hilarious and are similar to the submissions on *America's Funniest Home Videos*, if you are familiar with that show. Sometimes the people in the video laugh at themselves. Some videos, however, raise concerns.

There are some subcategories of these fail videos that should make us slow down and think about our response to them. A broad but age-old question to help us reflect is this: Am I laughing with the people in the video, or am I laughing at them?

Some of the subcategories of these videos include "cringe fails" or "awkward fails." I've seen plenty of these videos and even laughed at them. But I have times of deeper reflection when I think, *I'm watching real people experience something unpleasant and embarrassing*. If it was uncomfortable for them, should I take pleasure in it? Again, sometimes people may laugh at their own downfall, but sometimes they don't.

Some videos go beyond the fail category altogether and mock people in uncomfortable situations. For example, I personally think that airhorns are one of the funniest noises on the planet. I don't know why, but I laugh almost one hundred percent of the time when I hear an airhorn. You may be familiar with videos of people hiding around golf courses and blowing an airhorn in the middle of someone's backswing. The golfers jump, drop their golf clubs, look around in surprise and confusion. I have laughed at many of these videos.

At the same time, the golfers typically don't laugh. There are plenty of videos where the golfers get the joke and laugh, but there are far more where the golfers not only don't laugh, but get very, *very* angry. I've seen some angry golfers begin to chase the pranksters. Others have aimed their golf balls at the pranksters. And there are others who are too old to chase, so they just scream words I cannot repeat. Whatever the category, these golfers were just going about their day, trying to relax or improve their golf game when they are rudely disrupted. It's understandably frustrating. Should I laugh at this? Should I get joy from other people's misery? I want you to wrestle with those questions because I don't think laughing at these fails is loving others the way the opening verse encourages us to.

Loving Misery

Let's explore these concerns in the realm of texting and social media (YouTube is classified as social media, but I'm thinking of Instagram, TikTok, and similar apps). I think it's safe to say that many teenagers want hundreds of likes and followers. More likes and followers typically point to popularity and that's a good feeling for anyone.

There are some types of attention, however, that don't make you feel good. When you get hundreds of likes and comments mocking a picture someone posted of you. When everyone in your school comments on a video that made you look ugly or stupid. That type of attention hurts.

Consider this—a lot of our screen-watching is fictional. We stream movies all the time of make-believe people and places. Therefore, I think we sometimes forget that we're looking at real people on social media, and we detach ourselves from their feelings. We might not even realize that our sinful hearts are taking pleasure at another person's sadness and embarrassment.

At the same time, our sinful hearts do take joy in the misery of others. The cringy, awkward photo of someone in our class gives us some delight. The video of another classmate singing off-key makes us feel superior. That delight increases if it's someone who has made life difficult for us. We can take joy (a twisted, sinful joy) in their downfall. We can be so prideful and insensitive toward others, but what if this judgment is turned toward us? The threat of being judged, ridiculed, rejected, and basically unloved causes us to fear.

The opening verse tells us that perfect love drives out fear. If most of us are honest, there is a type of fear that's present anytime we post. No, it's not the kind of fear you associate with going through a haunted house, watching a horror movie, or walking through the woods alone at night. It's a sneakier fear, a subtle kind of anxiety we experience when our pictures or words go public. That anxiety might sound like . . .

- *What if no one likes what I post? What does that say about me?*
- *What if people make fun of the way I look?*
- *What if I've overlooked something embarrassing that others may see once I post?*
- *What if this group ignores what I post?*
- *Why did that person share the picture of me I asked them not to?*

The real fear of posting is found in the lack of love from others. We're afraid that we won't receive the love and affirmation that we want. As the verse tells us, fear is the opposite of love. But the reality of social media is that, because so many of you have experienced a lack of love in this context, fear is appropriate. Fear is something you expect.

While the love of Christ should challenge believers to love others, let's not jump past the fact that Christ loved us first. He loved us when we were his unloving, enemies. He tells us that his love is so strong for us that no one will snatch us out of his hands (John 10:27–30). It is out of the overflow of Christ's love for us that we are free to love others. It is this love that drives away our fear of how someone will receive our post. It may hurt us deeply when someone says something harmful about our picture, but let that fear drive you into the arms of Jesus.

Don't think this is an overnight change that will take place. This isn't always something that clicks like flipping a switch. It is, however, a powerful truth you need to speak back to yourself.

Now, understanding the love of Jesus, moves us outward to love others. How can you strive to perpetuate love through social media? Instead of sharing a viral video of someone being humiliated, how might you love the person on the other side of the screen—even if it's someone on the other side of the world that you may never meet?

And what if the person is someone you go to school with? What if an embarrassing picture goes around and everyone mocks them? How might you love that person? What sort of love from Jesus can you show to them? Jesus loved you in the midst of your shame and misery; how might you show that same love to others?

Loving others sounds so basic, but the older I get, I realize more and more how hard it is to love people. At the same time, the older I get, the more amazed I am at Jesus. How did Jesus love people so well? The obvious answer is the fact that he was, and is, the Son of God. But when we answer this way, we can lose sight of the humanity of Jesus. He had to deal with difficult, wicked, and hate-filled people, yet he still loved them.

Typically, the hate-filled characters from Scripture only expose our own hearts and the wickedness we're capable of. Don't despair, though. Jesus's love is greater than your wickedness. He loves to welcome repentant sinners like you and me.

Practice

Social media can perpetuate darkness, but as believers, we are called to strive to bring the light of Christ (including his love) to this area of our culture. Below are several suggestions for ways you can be a light for Christ through social media.

Ideas for spreading love through social media:

- Follow someone in your school that doesn't have a lot of followers.
- Post an encouraging comment on someone's picture.
- Give someone a shout-out through a post, reel, or story. Keep the focus on them and use specific, life-giving words to describe them.

- Don't just love people virtually. Speak to them in person with a word of encouragement, or a (genuine) compliment. Better yet, sit down and have a conversation with them, face-to-face. Love them by genuinely listening to them. Get to know who they are and what they like.
- Ask Jesus to help you refuse to join in when you see someone being embarrassed or mocked (whether in person or online).
- If someone shares an embarrassing photo of someone with you, just delete it. Don't spread it around.
- If you've made fun of someone (behind their back or not), let God convict you. Ask for his forgiveness (which he promises in 1 John 1:9). If you made fun of that person openly, ask God for courage to apologize openly.
- When you see someone being embarrassed or made fun of, whether you know them or not, stop to pray for them. Ask God to comfort and protect them. Ask him to convict those who are mocking them. Ask him to bring reconciliation and restoration.

SONG

"Coming Home" by Drew Holcomb and the Neighbors

DAY 3: JOY[1]

I am speaking the truth in Christ—I am not lying . . . . I have great sorrow and unceasing anguish in my heart. (Romans 9:1–2)

Rejoice in the Lord always; again I will say, rejoice. (Philippians 4:4)

Question

What brings you joy? When you look at how you spend most of your days, what do they reveal about your pursuit of joy? Maybe you spend most of your free time playing sports, trying to perfect an athletic skill by practicing the same play over and over until you practically collapse. Maybe you often find yourself hunched over a desk, poring over books and studying in your free time so you can get into your dream school. Maybe you spend afternoons and weekends in your room, playing video games, staring intensely at the screen and jamming buttons as you try to beat your best score.

It has been said that our calendars can reveal our idols. That is, what you spend the most time doing often reveals what you worship. Likewise, what you spend the most time doing often reveals what you find joy in—or, at the very least, what you attempt to find joy in. In the Scripture and story below, you'll see that sometimes joy can be elusive in this fallen world.

Scripture

Have you ever heard people say that they don't like the church because it's filled with hypocrites? We may get defensive, but I think we can admit that we're all hypocritical at times. The church is filled with sinners, so let's not try to hide that.

When we read the above verses and realize that they were both written by the apostle Paul, we may be tempted to call him a hypocrite or say he's contradicting himself. On the one hand, he says to rejoice always! Then, he says he has great sorrow and unceasing anguish. *How can you say both, Paul!?* Did he think the church in Rome wouldn't share what he said with the church in Philippi?

What are these verses trying to tell us? While Paul wrote these letters, we know God is the ultimate author of Scripture. And we also know from Scripture that God is incapable of lying, being hypocritical, and contradicting himself (Titus 1:2).

In the following story, we'll unpack this truth: joy can be found in this life, but it is often momentary, incomplete, and fleeting. Joy and sorrow can, and do, often exist together.

Story

Years ago, my wife and I celebrated our fifteenth anniversary in Seaside, Florida. If you've ever seen the old Jim Carrey movie *The Truman Show* (1998), it was filmed in Seaside, so that gives you some idea of what it looks like. For those who haven't seen the movie, it's a quaint, little town. There's an iconic market, restaurants and food trucks that smell amazing as you walk by. The architecture of the homes is so unique. Sometimes we'd take evening strolls and simply admire the unique homes and try to imagine what they look like on the inside. In short, it's a peaceful, idyllic location right by the ocean.

We had been to Seaside several times before this anniversary trip, so we knew what to expect. We were looking forward to several child-free days (we love our children) of relaxation, good food, and celebrating God's gift of our marriage. However, there are some things you just can't plan for.

On this particular visit, we discovered something called red tide. For those who are unfamiliar with red tide, the

National Oceanic and Atmospheric Administration describes it this way: "A red tide is an event that occurs on the coastline when algae . . . grows out of control."[2] While you can swim in red tide, it can be a hindrance to some people's breathing and cause mild skin irritation. The algae can cause the ocean to appear red, hence the name. I can affirm that description. It wasn't bloodred like I imagine the plague from Exodus was, but it seemed to have a red tint to it.

Unaware of this red tide, we packed snacks and made our way down to the beach. I sat there most of the day thinking I had gotten sunscreen in my eyes. They wouldn't stop burning and watering. Nothing extreme, but a mild annoyance. The next day, I experienced the same thing but a little worse—stinging, burning eyes. Then, it became unbearable for me to sit at the beach because of constant coughing and eyes that wouldn't stop watering. Dead sea life also began to wash up on the beach. An assortment of fish was strewn all along the shoreline—puffers, remoras (also known as suckerfish), and sea snakes.

We won't talk about the fact that the red tide didn't bother my wife like it did me (she's tougher than I am, okay?). I will say that I wasn't the only one at the pool for most of the week. More and more people left the beach due to the red tide. Yes, the red tide did take away some of the joy of our beach trip, but we still had a great time.

True Joy

Have you ever had something like this happen to you? Maybe not red tide, but have you made plans to do something you take joy in, only to have it thwarted? You go on a long-awaited family vacation, only to end up with food poisoning that strands you on the lumpy couch of the vacation rental while the rest of your family goes out. You get tickets to your favorite artist, but the seats are way in the back, so you have to stand on your toes and crane your neck, the singer looking like an ant from where you're standing. Joy is often elusive in a fallen world. To be sure, we find it most days, but even when we do, it can be short lived.

If we find joy in something, chances are that we will want more of whatever it is. If joy is the beach, then we'll go to the beach until our hands and feet are all wrinkly from being in the ocean. If it's the mountains, off we go, hiking any weekend we can and investing in fancy outdoor gear. If it's ice cream, then we'll fill our freezers so we can have easy access to it—chocolate fudge, cookie dough, cake batter, you name it. Nature, sports, movies—we will find a way to pursue the things that bring us joy with as much frequency as we're able. Prioritizing these things and spending lots of time on them becomes easy because we love them and see them as a source of joy.

And if frequency is an indicator of what we find joy in, then we might conclude that we believe our phones are a source of joy. It's likely you've found yourself unlocking your phone and swiping to your favorite app without even thinking about it. Some of us use our phones to help with homework or for business, so joy might not always be the reason we use them frequently. For many, though, our phones play a vital role in our search for joy, whether it's from that long-awaited response from our crush, another funny reel on social media, or more likes, comments, and re-shares from our recent posts.

According to one study, the average American checks their phone 344 times a day, or once every 4 minutes.[3] Once again, not every pickup of the device inherently indicates a search for joy, but some do. A quick scroll on Instagram is often a quest for joy. Before you disagree, consider this. Would you pick your phone up if it was an absolutely miserable experience? I would imagine that you would reach for it less and less if that were the case.

When the day has been long and we're ready to prop our feet up and relax, we often reach for our devices first. Why? They're an escape from the fallen world we inhabit. What are we escaping from? Pain, difficulty, sadness, boredom. What are we trying to escape to? Comfort, ease, and joy. Phones allow us to disengage from our thoughts and become mere consumers.

I'm sure many will point to the chemicals in our brains as a major reason why we pick up our phones. The rush of dopamine we get from someone liking our picture or giving us a follow or a mention feels like joy in the moment. However, the fleeting nature of this feeling seems to indicate that this isn't true joy. Also, many admit that they actually feel worse when they get off of social media than they did when they first got on. Nevertheless, the hope of finding joy—however trivial and short-lived—keeps people coming back for more.

Fighting for Joy

So how do you find true joy? Well, true joy takes time. It involves effort. True joy is even found through pain. We, however, often want quick hits of laughter, cheerfulness, and levity, which can be short lived. I am not saying this is all bad, but I want you to see and believe that biblical joy offers something deeper, something eternal.

A Christian's ultimate joy is tied to the salvation Jesus Christ accomplished for us. This is why Paul can tell Christians to "rejoice in the Lord always; again I will say, rejoice" (Philippians 4:4). Christians, Jesus has won an unfading joy that cannot be taken away by anything! If that doesn't move your heart to rejoice, pray that it would. Fight for it!

However, if true joy is tied to the salvation we have in Jesus, there's a sense in which we will never have true joy until we leave this world and go home to be with our Savior. I am not saying that we cannot have joy or that we don't get glimpses and tastes of true joy in this life. It's just that we will not fully experience joy until we're at home with Jesus. In short, this world isn't our home.

In addition, many of us—myself included—look for joy in the wrong things and miss our Creator's goodness in the things we enjoy. I often enjoy things in this world and forget to acknowledge the grace of my Creator's fingerprints that are all over those things. Things like cookies, movies, music, times with friends, and every other good thing God has given us. We can find joy in all of those things, but that joy pales in comparison to what awaits us in the next life. It would be a good idea to list your top three, five, or ten favorite things to do and then turn those into a prayer of thanksgiving to God, who is the giver of every good gift.

The Enemy of Joy

What gets in the way of our joy? The easy answer: sin. My own sin keeps me from joy. It keeps me from acknowledging the good things God has given me. It keeps me looking for joy in empty ways. It tells me that chocolate chip cookies are the most incredible creation, so I scarf down too many and then feel worse. It convinces me that one more YouTube video will give me what I'm looking for, some humor, levity, inspiration, encouragement, distraction from my burdens and to-dos. *Just a little more scrolling and you'll find it.*

I think our search for ultimate joy in the wrong things contributes to the sadness we experience from social media. We pick up our devices searching for this joy, but we come away from them with emptiness. One thing I want you to realize is that many of our pursuits for joy in this life are simply shallow. Maybe you often feel joyless after your time on social media because it's a fairly joyless activity to begin with. In fact, it can fuel the discontentment, anxiety, pride, and covetousness that's already in our hearts, leaving us feeling worse.

When you really think about it, how much joy can a place like Instagram offer? It's a place that constantly reminds you that you're not popular enough. And, even if you are popular, popularity cannot give you lasting, true joy. It's a place that reminds you that your day wasn't as good as someone else's. You're not as athletic. Not as beautiful. Not as smart or gifted. Not as accomplished. Not as liked. Not as . . .

Social media isn't designed to foster joy. It's a place that reveals our idols, our fruitless endeavors for notoriety, and our vanity. When we receive these things—notoriety for our accomplishments, talents, or looks—they're still not enough. We always want more. In short, social media reveals longing, and longing reveals the fact that we aren't home.

My goal isn't to tell you to leave social media, but to make you aware of your pursuit for joy through social media, and to point you toward the source of real joy: Christ Jesus himself. Yes, it's unrealistic to think that Christians will walk around with constant smiles on our faces, clapping our hands, and dancing because of what Jesus did for us. Know that sadness and longing are to be expected. But the joys of this life give us glimpses of the next life, the eternal life that Jesus bought for us. And it's the reality of that next life that can shape the way we look at social media today. Instead of expecting social media to deliver lasting joy, we can enjoy it for what it is (a gift from God), use it wisely and well, and let our unfulfilled longings prompt us to run to Jesus for perfect, lasting joy.

Practice

In Psalm 51, David asks God, "Restore to me the joy of your salvation" (verse 12a). When was the last time you took joy in the salvation of Jesus? I'm not guilt-tripping you with that question. I fail at this too! Seriously though, do you take joy in the salvation you have? Below is a list of some of what Christians can take joy in. If you don't yet know Jesus, know that the following things can be true for you if you turn toward Christ (and therefore away from sin), asking him to save you and give you a new heart. Ask God to open your eyes and help you embrace him if you haven't yet. And if you have, ask him to open your eyes to see and believe how great this gift of salvation and joy is.

- All your sins—past, present, and future—have been paid for.
- Jesus has given you his perfect righteousness.
- God the Father smiles at you as his beloved child.
- You have the Holy Spirit as a Helper in your fight against sin.
- No struggle or sin you have (or will *ever* have) is stronger than God's grace.
- You are loved and accepted by God, always!
- There's a day coming when it will be *impossible* for you to sin.
- A day of true rest from all your anxiety and depression is coming.
- The new heavens and earth will be a place where all your fears are gone.
- All of this, and more than we can imagine, will last forever.

SONG

"Praise to the Lord the Almighty" by Sara Groves (or favorite artist rendition)

Take note of this lyric, "Ponder anew what the Almighty can do."

DAY 4: PEACE

If possible, so far as it depends on you, live peaceably with all. (Romans 12:18)

Question

If you could describe your perfect day, what would it consist of? If you could have one free day to do whatever you wanted (that wasn't sinful or illegal), what would you do? Take some time to think about that now. Lounge on the beach? Have an all-day shopping excursion? Play your favorite video game in a plush recliner to your heart's content? Sleep until the afternoon? Don't hold back. Write your answers down if you want. Write them in this book.

After you come up with some ideas, reflect on them. What do they reveal about you? Your wants and desires? Do they reveal a self-focused heart? Do they reveal a heart of service? This can be an eye-opening exercise.

Regardless of what you wrote, these questions point us to a core truth of Christianity: you were created for unshakeable peace and perfection. This desire is woven into our hearts from Eden, but it's still there even after sin entered the world because we long to be home with Jesus. The desire for peace deeply resonates in our hearts.

Scripture

It's probably safe to say that most of the encouragements in Scripture imply that the opposite is a possibility as well. Consider the opening verse. If Paul is telling us to "live peaceably," it's because the opposite is our reality. He must tell us to live peaceably because strife is natural in this fallen world;

peace is not. The divisiveness we see about politics today is one example. You don't have to surf the internet or watch the news for long to see people going at each other with hate-filled remarks and arrogant comments about their views. People shake their heads in arrogance, call each other names, roll their eyes, or use multiple angry face emojis while communicating with people who disagree with them. Maybe you even see this kind of division at your own dinner table with your family. Living peaceably isn't going to be easy because division and difficulty are common.

Even though difficulty is to be expected in our relationships with others, Paul doesn't remove the burden of peace as a responsibility of believers. The phrase, "so far as it depends on you," tells us that striving for peace is something we can pursue or avoid.

As we will see from the story below, there is outward and inward peace. Outward peace involves peaceable actions we can perform, but inner peace exists between us and Jesus.

Story

At a conference, I once heard pastor and author Kevin DeYoung state the following idea: "Reading blog comments for edification is like sticking your head in the toilet looking for gummy bears."[1]

If you have no idea what he's talking about, you've probably never read the comment section on social media platforms. Some of the most vile, hurtful, and divisive statements are made there. These forums are typically fairly anonymous, and anonymity often brings out the worst in people. Peace is rarely found there.

When visiting the comment section, you may come across "trolls." For those who don't know what a troll is, one online computer literacy training program defines it as "a person who intentionally tries to instigate conflict, hostility, or arguments in an online social community. Platforms targeted by trolls can include the comment sections of YouTube, forums, or chat rooms."[2] These people make divisive comments to elicit a reaction and stir up strife.

A troll does the opposite of Romans 12:18. Dare I say, a troll lives in your heart and mine. When we witness a troll online, it might bring a smirk to our faces—not only because a troll can say truly funny things, but because there is part of our fallen heart that likes conflict, hostility, and arguments. So we pull up a virtual seat to this online boxing match like we're at the movies, shoving popcorn in our mouths as we eagerly wait for the show to begin. We're here to enjoy the conflict. Maybe it sinfully fuels our sense of superiority in not being the ones commenting. Whatever the reason, our tendency to entertain division and conflict should grieve us. Seeds of rebellion are in every fallen human heart, so we understand why trolls exist.

Therefore, the obvious application of this chapter is this: *don't be a troll and don't find joy in other trolls.* But I also want to take us beyond this in just a bit.

In the latter section of this portion from Romans, we read, "do not be overcome by evil, but overcome evil with good" (Romans 12:21). Maybe we could say "don't be overcome by your *trollness*, but overcome your *trollness* with good." Be someone who creates peace through your posts. Not only by what you post, but also in your interactions with what others post—even if your interactions are anonymous. Remember the first chapter of this book: God is omnipresent; he sees and knows your comments, and the heart behind them, even if others online don't.

Christians are to be salt and light in this world, which includes social media. Consider some of the other encouragements Paul gives in this section of Romans 12:

- Abhor (hate) what is evil (verse 9b).
- Hold fast to what is good (verse 9c).
- Outdo one another in showing honor (verse 10b).

- Rejoice with those who rejoice (verse 15a).
- Weep with those who weep (verse 15b).
- Repay no one evil for evil (verse 17a).

Paul says more, but could you imagine if everyone on social media attempted to live by the above encouragements? I would assume that the vast majority of human beings—Christian or otherwise—would agree that these words of Paul are some good ones to live by.

As believers, we need to be reminded that Paul grounds these encouragements in the gospel. In other words, Jesus lived the sort of life these verses describe, and he paid for all the ways you've failed to live that life. Now live out what Jesus has accomplished on your behalf. We don't live peaceably in order to *earn* God's favor; we live peaceably because God has *given* us his favor through Christ. Our gracious lifestyle is lived out of thanksgiving to the grace that has been shown to us in Jesus.

Inward Peace

We should be encouraged to pursue a peaceful lifestyle through our online interactions, but there is another application; one that might not be as obvious. You see, you can convey peace externally, through your texts, comments, and posts, but still not have peace *internally*.

For example, have you ever "liked" a picture of a friend, but not really liked it in your heart?

Consider this example: You see a picture of your friend and immediately have a negative feeling. Maybe you're sad because you don't feel like you're as loved as they are, as beautiful as they are, as fit as they are, and so on. Maybe they posted a photo with their significant other, smiling and looking so happy, which tempts you to feel inferior . . . or jealous . . . or discontent as a single person. Whatever the scenario may be, their picture made you feel bad. But even though the picture left a negative impression on you, you "liked" it anyway.

Why did you do this? You liked their picture because . . .

- You knew they would notice if you didn't like it.
- They're popular and you wanted to stay on their good side.
- You wanted to earn their "like" when you post something.
- Fill in the blank . . .

Perhaps you were sad, but you liked their picture just to be nice. That's a real possibility and that gets at the exact thing Paul is saying: "If possible, so far as it depends on you, live peaceably with all." You're striving by grace to create peace.

You may like their picture for various reasons, *but you don't really like it in your heart*. To be honest, the picture made you sad, mad, jealous, or any other emotion that wouldn't fall in the category of . . . like. Negative emotions like these, and many others, swirl around in our hearts, creating distress.

This final week of devotions has to do with *fighting* these heart-level battles. We're digging into the heart and asking the Spirit to grow us into the image of Jesus. By the power of the Holy Spirit, we fight to live out our identity as Christians. Dallas Willard once said, "Grace is opposed to earning, not to the effort we put forth after we receive it."[3] We do not earn what Christ bought by his blood, but we do exert ourselves to live in a manner worthy of the gospel of Christ (Philippians 1:27; 2:12–13).

You must make an effort in the fight for inner peace, making war with the troll that lives inside you. More specifically, you must fight the inner voices you hear as you're scrolling, the manipulative voices you listen to more than you might realize. Consider how some of these inner voices speak to you:

- *Delay a response to their text message. That way you won't appear needy.*

- *Don't "like" their picture, so you can remain in a position of power over them.*
- *Post a picture of your friend group to feel superior.*
- *Intentionally leave someone untagged in your picture.*
- *Post this smiling picture of yourself to make people think you're happy.*
- *Post this to make others envious of what you have or what you're doing.*

Some of these have been temptations of my own heart that I've acted on at times. I've also had these common thoughts confirmed to me by others. I'm confident that many reading this have dealt with at least one of these thoughts, but I'm sure they have many more they could share. What are the inner voices of your heart saying?

Moving Toward Peace

It is easy to see that social media is tarnished with much wickedness. There is so much hurt perpetuated through various platforms. As you have seen, the real root of the evils of social media is found in the human heart. Our own heart makes so much of our technology anything but peaceful.

The first step in fighting for peace on a heart level is realizing it's not natural. Your heart isn't bent toward peace. It's restless, fearful, angry, and divisive. And social media churns up so much fear in your heart.

Not only is this realization vital in your fight, but prayer is too. Christians cannot possibly fight apart from the strength of the Spirit, so we must pray. This might sound strange, but it would be a good idea to say a prayer before you get on social media. If prayer is not a common practice for your time on social media, maybe this is what's hindering your peace. Pray Colossians 3:15, that by God's grace you would "let the peace of Christ rule in your hearts."

The knowledge of our broken hearts and the power of prayer are vital, but taking action is the third step toward peace. Taking action looks like doing the opposite of what your heart typically tells you. The world often tells us to follow our hearts, but that's typically the worst advice you could ever live by. Remember Jeremiah 17:9? Our hearts are "deceptive," and "desperately sick."

In other words:

- Don't follow your heart when you're tempted to intentionally leave someone untagged from your picture.
- Don't follow your heart when you want to manipulate someone by texting or not texting them, or intentionally delaying your response when you can respond sooner.
- Don't follow your heart when you want to make someone jealous by what you post.
- Don't follow your heart when you want to post an image to get others to worship you.

I encourage you to act through social media in ways that will foster peace both online *and* in your heart. You see, when you start playing the manipulation game, you create inner turmoil. You have turmoil as you debate what to post or not post, but then you begin to project those thoughts onto other people's posts. You begin to have paranoia toward everyone else and the *possible* motives behind what they share. So, you end up lacking peace in your own heart by not fostering peace through what you post.

In summary, know that your heart isn't naturally inclined toward peace, pray that you'll have peace as you interact online, and foster peace by acting in love toward others.

Practice

If you're reading this, then you've made it to the end of this devotional (unless you skipped ahead). Good job! Seriously, completing an entire book is an accomplishment and you should take a moment to thank the Lord for giving you the ability to finish a book. Way to go! And thank you.

I sincerely pray that the Lord uses this book to grow your love for Jesus and give you wisdom to use social media in a God-honoring way.

For this practice, I want to ask you to reflect on this book as a whole. Close it. Look at the cover. Turn it to the side and look at the thickness of it. Reflect on all those pages you read. After you do that, flip back through the book and look at some underlined portions or maybe pages you folded. If there's anything that stood out to you, take one more look at it before you put this book back on the shelf.

Maybe turn some of those underlined portions into prayers. Take some of the practices that were the most helpful and continue to use them in some way.

Lastly, go out to eat with your Alongsider. If you're able, offer to pay for their meal. Thank them for the investment they made in your life. For the time they've given to you. Spend some time reflecting on this book, but also spend some time asking them how they're doing. See if there's a way you could pray for them. Then, if you are comfortable doing so, spend some time praying out loud for them and thank God for putting them in your life.

SONG

"God's Highway" by Sandra McCracken

THE WEEKEND CONVERSATION

1. Which day stuck out to you the most and why?
   - ❐ HEART
   - ❐ LOVE
   - ❐ JOY
   - ❐ PEACE

2. Did you learn anything new about yourself by asking yourself "why?" all week?

3. Reflect on an experience where you felt fully seen and truly loved. What was that like? Are you able to experience or give that kind of genuine love through social media? Why or why not?

4. Were you able to start thinking about and/or experiencing the joy of your salvation in a new way this week?

5. Which of the Practices did you enjoy most? Which helped you to connect with Jesus?

6. Which song and/or lyric did you most resonate with? Why?

7. How can your Alongsider be praying for you?

ENDNOTES

Week 1

Day 1

1. Not his real name.

Day 2

1. Jean M. Twenge, "Have Smartphones Destroyed a Generation?" *The Atlantic*, September 2017, https://www.theatlantic.com/magazine/archive/2017/09/has-the-smartphone-destroyed-a-generation/534198/.

Day 4

1. Sarah Eekhoff Zylstra, "Scrolling Alone: How Instagram Is Making a Generation of Girls, Lonely, Anxious, and Sad," July 20, 2022 in *Recorded*, produced by Josh Diaz, podcast, 46:41, https://www.thegospelcoalition.org/podcasts/recorded/scrolling-alone/.

Week 2

Day 2

1. Melissa Kruger and Sarah Zylstra, "Rested Development (A. J. Swaboda) & Social Sanity in an Insta World (Melissa Kruger & Sarah Zylstra," May 16, 2022, episode 358 in *The Local Youth Worker*, produced by RYM, podcast, 1:05:24, https://thelocalyouthworker.podbean.com/e/358-rested-development-aj-swaboda-social-sanity-in-an-insta-world-melissa-kruger-sarah-zylstra/.

Day 4

1. Helen Thorne, "Biblical Sexuality, Pornography & Women (Helen Thorne)," May 10, 2021, episode 330 in *The Local Youth Worker*, produced by RYM, podcast, 38:32, https://thelocalyouthworker.podbean.com/e/episode-330-biblical-sexuality-pornography-women-helen-thorne/.

2. Helen Thorne, *Purity Is Possible: How to Live Free of the Fantasy Trap* (Epsom, England: The Good Book Company, 2014), 7–8.

Week 3

Day 1

1. *#Being13: Inside the Secret World of Teens*, a CNN Special Report, directed by Eli Lazar, featuring Anderson Cooper, Robert Faris, and Marion Underwood, aired October 6, 2015, on CNN, 42:55, https://www.imdb.com/title/tt6529880/.

2. Edward T. Welch, *Addictions: A Banquet in the Grave* (Phillipsburg, NJ: P&R Publishing, 2001), xvi.

Day 2

1. Jean M. Twenge, *iGen: Why Today's Super-Connected Kids Are Growing Up Less Rebellious, More Tolerant, Less Happy—and Completely Unprepared for Adulthood* (New York: Atria, 2017); Adam Altar, *Irresistible: The Rise of Addictive Technology and the Business of Keeping Us Hooked* (New York: Penguin, 2018); Tony Reinke, *12 Ways Your Phone Is Changing You* (Wheaton: Crossway, 2017); Andy Crouch, *The Tech-Wise Family* (Grand Rapids: Baker, 2017).

2. *Pocket Dictionary of Theological Terms*, by Stanley J. Grenz, David Guretzki, and Cherith Fee Nordling (Downers Grove: InterVarsity Press), s.v. "sin."

Day 3

1. Auke de Vries, *The Super Rope Solution*, animated short, 4:46, accessed August 2022, https://www.youtube.com/watch?v=HAyN2HKJpKA.

2. *The Social Dilemma*, a Netflix Original Documentary, directed by Jeff Orlowski (Boulder, CO: Exposure Labs, 2020), https://www.netflix.com/watch/81254224.

3. *The Social Dilemma*, 45:50.

4. Chris Martin, "5 New Stats You Should Know About Teens and Social Media," *The Gospel Coalition*, August 11, 2022, https://www.thegospelcoalition.org/article/stats-teens-social/.

Day 4

1. *The Sixth Sense*, directed by M. Night Shyamalan (Burbank, CA: Hollywood Pictures, 1999), 107 min.

2. *Spider-Man: Into the Spider-verse*, directed by Bob Persichetti, Peter Ramsey, and Rodney Rothman (Culver City, CA: Columbia Pictures, 2018), 117 min.

Week 4

Day 1

1. J. C. Ryle, *Expository Thoughts on Matthew* (Edinburgh: Banner of Truth Trust, 2012), 40.

Day 3

1. While there is much original thought in this chapter, portions were impacted by a specific podcast from *Ask Pastor John*, Episode 840. I wanted to be sure to give credit to that resource. John Piper, "Do We Have Joy or Fight For It?", April 19, 2016 in *Ask Pastor John*, produced by desiringGod.org, podcast, 10:12, https://www.desiringgod.org/interviews/do-we-have-joy-or-fight-for-it.

2. "What Is a Red Tide," NOAA SciJinks, NOAA, accessed August 2022, https://scijinks.gov/red-tide/.

3. Trevor Wheelwright, "2022 Cell Phone Use Statistics: How Obsessed Are We," *Reviews.org*, January 24, 2022, https://www.reviews.org/mobile/cell-phone-addiction/.

Day 4

1. Kevin De Young, "Can We Be Glorified Without Being Sanctified? Good Works, Good News, and Christian

Assurance," (sermon, T4G Conference 2016, Louisville, KY, April 11–13, 2016), 29:03, https://t4g.org/resources/kevin-deyoung/asl-can-glorified-without-sanctified-good-works-good-news-christian-assurance/.

2. "What Is Trolling?" *The Now* (blog), GCFGlobal.org, accessed August 4, 2022, https://edu.gcfglobal.org/en/thenow/what-is-trolling/1/.

3. Dallas Willard, *The Great Omission: Reclaiming Jesus's Essential Teachings on Discipleship* (San Francisco: HarperCollins, 2006), 61.

Reformed Youth Ministries (RYM) exists to reach and equip students for Christ. Passing the faith on to the next generation has been RYM's passion since it began. In 1972 three youth workers who shared a passion for biblical teaching to youth surveyed the landscape of youth ministry conferences. What they found was an emphasis on fun and games, not God's Word. Therefore, they started a conference that focused on the preaching and teaching of God's Word. Over the years RYM has grown beyond conferences into three areas of ministry: conferences, training, and resources.

If you are passionate for passing the faith on to the next generation, please visit www.rym.org to learn more about Reformed Youth Ministries. If you are interested in partnering with us in ministry, please visit www.rym.org/donate.